KU-512-817

‘Cottage Pie’, by Fred Roe, R.I.

English Cottage Furniture

BY F. GORDON ROE

Henry Bright of the Norwich School.

Charles Bentley, Member of the 'Old Water-Colour' Society.

Dictator of the Royal Academy (Joseph Farington, R.A.).

David Cox.

Sporting Prints of the Eighteenth and Early Nineteenth Centuries.

Coronation Cavalcade

The Life and Times of King Edward VIII.

The Nude from Cranach to Etty and beyond.

The Bronze Cross.

Cox the Master.

English Period Furniture: An Introductory Guide.

Rowlandson: The Life and Art of a British Genius.

Old English Furniture from Tudor to Regency.

Sea Painters of Britain (2 Vols.).

Jointly

A Catalogue of the Pictures and Drawings in the Collection of Frederick John Nettlefold (with C. Reginald Grundy).

Etty and the Nude (with William Gaunt).

English Cottage Furniture

BY

F. GORDON ROE

Fellow of the Society of Antiquaries of London

Fellow of the Royal Historical Society

Sometime Editor of *The Connoisseur*

Phoenix House Limited

LONDON

Made 1949 in Great Britain
at Liverpool, Lancs., by C. Tinling & Co. Ltd. for
PHOENIX HOUSE LIMITED
38 William IV Street, London, W.C.2.

First published 1949

TO
THE DEAR MEMORY OF
MY MOTHER

LETITIA MABEL ROE

WHO DIED IN 1940 AS BRAVELY
AS SHE HAD LIVED
and of
MY FATHER

FRED ROE, R.I., R.B.C.

(1864-1947)
ARTIST IN PAINT AND WORDS,
A GREAT PIONEER OF THE
STUDY OF OLD OAK FURNITURE,
THIS BOOK
WHICH OWES SO MUCH TO THEM
IS DEDICATED
IN LOVE AND RESPECT

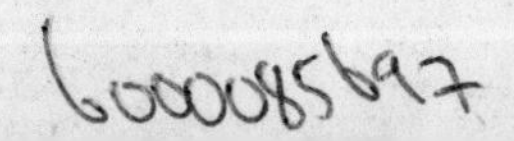

Acknowledgment

Grateful thanks are recorded to all who have in any way contributed to the writing and illustration of this book, among them the following: Mr F. S. Andrus (College of Arms), Dr Charles R. Beard, my cousin Miss Grace Belton, Mr Adrian Bury, Mr Desmond Butler, the Chapter of the College of Arms, Mr and Mrs Peter Desborough, Mr H. Granville Fell (Editor of *The Connoisseur*), Colonel J. C. Wynne Finch of Voelas, Sir Cyril Fox, P.P.S.A., (formerly Director of the National Museum of Wales, Cardiff), Mr C. H. Gibbs-Smith (Keeper of Museum Extension, Victoria and Albert Museum), Major Hugh Giffard and Mrs Hugh Giffard (Miss Iris Brooke, A.R.C.A.), Mr H. E. Goodchild, Mr Sidney S. Harris (Messrs M. Harris & Sons), the late Mrs Nevill Jackson, Mr William Jennings (Editor of *Apollo*), Rev. J. F. W. Leigh, F.Z.S., Colonel Manvers Meadows, D.S.O., F.S.A., Miss Grizel Maxwell, Mr L. John Mayes (Borough Librarian, High Wycombe), Miss Cecelia Neville, Mr Charles Partridge, F.S.A., the late Rev. Wm. C. Pearson (formerly Vicar of Henley, Suffolk), Dr Iorwerth C. Peate, F.S.A. (Keeper, Welsh Folk Museum, St Fagan's Castle, Cardiff), Mr Amyas Phillips (Messrs Phillips of Hitchin Ltd.), Rev. E. Ellis Roberts (Rector of Monks Risborough), my cousin Lord Swinfen, Mr J. R. Fawcett Thompson, Mr Anthony Richard Wagner, F.S.A., Richmond Herald, Messrs F. Weatherhead & Son Ltd, Rev. J. Gower Williams (Rector of Princes Risborough), Miss Alice Winchester (Editor of *Antiques*, New York City), Mr. S. W. Wolsey (Messrs S. W. Wolsey Ltd); and to my wife and daughter for their aid in coping with the chores inseparable from authorship.

It is but fair to Richmond Herald and to his colleagues of the College of Arms to add that though my remarks on the 'Coffers of Cope' in Chapter III are based on material courteously furnished by them, they are not responsible for my deductions from that material.

Acknowledgment is made to all who have permitted the reproduction of photographs. In all cases the copyrights of such photographs are reserved to the respective owners.

This book has been written much more from experience than from textula reference, but a number of literary acknowledgments are made in the text and notes. The following articles written by me for *Antiques* (New York) may aslo be mentioned: *Old Brass Candlesticks* (June 1938); *Door Porters in Brass and Iron* (October 1938); *Old Metal Fenders* (April 1939); *In the Likeness of Books* (February 1940); *Some Early Andirons* (October 1941). Various articles by my father, the late Fred Roe, R.I., in *The Connoisseur*, *Apollo*, and *The Antique Collector* have been re-read, and use made of details from the following books from his pen: *Ancient Coffers and Cupboards* (1902), *Old Oak Furniture* (1905; 2nd ed. 1908), *A History of Oak Furniture* (1920), *Ancient Church Chests and Chairs in the Home Counties round Greater London* (1929), *Essex Survivals* (1929).

F.G.R.

Foreword

IN his second series of *Collections and Recollections*, the late Right Hon. George W. E. Russell entertainingly reminded us of a gossip-column paragraph of a sort familiar to, at any rate, my older readers. It was to the effect that the Duke and Duchess of Bumbledom had left Bumbledom Abbey for their beautifully situated '*cottage ornée*', built at a cost of £100,000, with 'forty miles of grass drives in the grounds'.

Let me say at once that, in discussing English Cottage Furniture, I am not concerned with any such expensive nonsense as the '*cottage ornée*', which bears about as much relation to actual cottage-life as did Marie-Antoinette's *laiterie* at the Petit Trianon to genuine dairy-work. My theme is antique furniture such as was used—and is still usable—in true English cottages and farmsteads, as well as in such other types of dwelling as respond to the less exalted forms of traditional equipment.

Such is the demand for antique furniture that an average buyer's chances of making lucky 'finds' for next to nothing have been gravely diminished. Good old country chairs still procurable for a matter of shillings when I was a boy may now command as many pounds in the antique shops, and rarer items have proportionately waxed in value. All the same, it is still possible to furnish with antique country pieces on a relatively low outlay: certainly much lower than if one indulges one's taste with more magnificent classes of antiquity.

It is very far from my purpose to decry by implication the desirability of buying 'the best', so far as one's means or opportunities permit. Usually, the best in quality is also the best bargain, provided one does not buy at outrageous prices—outrageous, that is, in relation to the excellence or rarity of individual items. Figuratively speaking, the highest quality is at the top of the tree, so far as prices are concerned, though vagaries of taste may enable a knowing collector to make a 'good buy' simply because an excellent piece of furniture is of a sort not at the time in first demand. When

I was a boy, the emphasis in furniture-collecting was perhaps mainly on oak; at the moment of writing, it is on walnut, mahogany, satinwood, and such rare woods as sabicu, padouk, zebrawood, and so forth. This is the broadest generalization, but it serves to illustrate one of the various reasons why some admittedly rare and desirable types command a less value than others. It also indicates how the collector of country furniture may have a slight advantage over his more fastidious rivals in that he or she is largely, though not entirely, concerned with unfashionable woods. To a great extent, country furniture, when not made of that very pleasing material, honest English oak, brings in such other woods as beech, elm, yew, and a number of others, not forgetting fruit-woods, all possessed of individuality and charm.

It must not be supposed that antique country furniture is necessarily low-grade stuff of no importance. If we need a modern comparison with this, one of the best ways of finding it is to visit a somewhat remote village in Buckinghamshire, where Mr H. E. Goodchild still produces Windsor chairs which for style, elegance and finish are more than equal to many of the most polished performances of the past. I shall have more to say on this point, but it should be emphasized here that just as town furniture has its degrees of quality, so too have its country cousins. It is incorrect to assert a single standard of quality throughout the length and breadth of furniture-collecting. Nor is there any need to wax superior about the claims of 'wealthy' or 'aristocratic' furniture as opposed to the less showy varieties which, for the most part, served the needs of our rural ancestors. Here, again, there are degrees of quality. If, in the main, it was the expensive town furniture that set the fashion, country-made pieces not infrequently show an individuality of treatment that renders them of interest. Here, we may say, was truly the furniture of the people: a detail which alone should render it of moment in a nominally democratic age.

Despite the obvious merit of much country furniture, the literature wholly devoted to it is somewhat scanty. Many books allude to it or incidentally illustrate examples, but of works *on* country-made furniture there are few enough. The late Arthur Hayden's *Chats on Cottage and Farmhouse Furniture* (originally published in 1912) gave a pioneering lead, and, though she rarely commits herself to a date, there is useful material in Gertrude Jekyll's *Old English Household Life* (1925). Certain other sources will be remembered by the careful student of such matters. In the present volume is essayed a new approach to the subject: an approach which, in the general reader's interest, avoids the higher technicalities, and, while giving such data as may be of direct utility, does not ignore the essentially human interest of an essentially 'human' theme.

Finally, in choosing the illustrations, I have been a good deal actuated by the desirability of showing things such as 'can be got' rather than by attempting the impossibility of representing every type that may occur. A few rarities are, however, included for the sake of the light they shed on less important pieces of equivalent period.

Here, then, we find ourselves at the cottage—or small country-house-door : a dream-cottage for some of us, perhaps, but none the less something to look forward to. Let us enter and listen to the tale that each of the grave old bits of furniture about the rooms has got to tell us, if only we have the wit to catch their meaning.

Wayside,
Princes Risborough.

F. GORDON ROE

Contents

Illustrations

FRONTISPIECE · *Cottage Pie*
From an original water-colour sketch by Fred Roe, R.I., R.B.C. (1864-1947). The artist has chosen to show a long Table of Gothic type. The chairs are Windsors, including a plain stick-back variety; and a funnel-shaped muller of copper hangs from the chimney-beam.

FIRST GROUP OF PLATES BETWEEN PAGES 32 AND 33

FIG. 1—*Dr Syntax turned Nurse*, by Thomas Rowlandson. This drawing was aquatinted in 1820, but gives in the main an excellent idea of a farmhouse kitchen of earlier date. Some of the furniture is certainly eighteenth-century, and the hanging spice-cupboard might be even older. Note ladder-back chairs and basket-work cradle; also warming-pan hanging beside doorway, and harvester's keg on shelf of the fitted dresser nearby. *Photo by courtesy of Mr V. Philip Sabin.*

FIG. 2—Small 'Boarded Chest' of oak ('coffer-type'; width 24½ in.), a late fifteenth- early sixteenth-century example of a long-enduring method. Note 'flush' construction, and slab-ends with 'buttressed' fore-edges. The lid, however, is modern and of incorrect design. *Author's Collection.*

FIG. 3—Plain oak Chest of framed construction, *provenance* unknown, seventeenth century. It retains its original key which has jammed in the lock and thus been preserved. The relatively tall and narrow panels represent a traditional 'hang-over' from earlier times. *Belonging to Miss Grace Belton.*

FIG. 4—Travelling Trunk of stained wood, ornamented with brass-headed nails, initialled and dated EH 1685 and believed to have belonged to a family named Harmon. It retains its original block-printed lining paper (seen below), showing groups of figures in the dress of the period. A flap in the base of the trunk gives access to drawers. From the neighbourhood of Speen, Bucks, and now in the Museum, Aylesbury, Bucks. *Photos by courtesy of Mr Desmond Butler.*

FIG. 5—Large oak Chest of framed construction, with ownership initials and date IW (16)95, the work throughout being of traditional and unmodish character. Such slightly carved pieces are sometimes spoilt by further carving, added in modern times in an effort to enhance their saleability. *Belonging to Mrs F. Gordon Roe.*

FIG. 6—Oak Boxes of so-called 'Bible-Box' type. *Above*: The carved front sixteenth-century, but the rest of the box, though anciently assembled, is early seventeenth. Width 17¾ in. Bought at Colchester, Essex. *Below*: Commonwealth box dated 1652, here shown without its modern lid. Width 28¾ in. (*Ex coll. Townroe*). *Both in the Author's Collection.* (*Photos by courtesy of 'The Connoisseur'*).

FIG. 7—Oak Table Desk or 'Desk-Box' dated 1682 and with an uncarved space reserved for ownership initials. The desk retains most of its original metal furniture. *Author's Collection.* (*Photo by courtesy of 'Apollo'*).

FIG. 8—Club or Tavern Tobacco-Box of oak, earlier part of the eighteenth century, 9 in. high, 12 in. long, 7 in. deep: an unusual item in wood and of this size and period. It is operated by pressing a coin through a slot in one of the twin lids. Beneath is an oak Joined Stool of about the second quarter of the seventeenth century; its rails and feet are missing, and the stool is seen as it was found in the neighbourhood of Speen, Bucks, where it was helping to support the Trunk in Fig. 4. *Photo by courtesy of Mr Desmond Butler; the Stool is in the Author's Collection.*

FIG. 9—Oak Armchair, *temp.* Elizabeth, initialled WB, and signed with maker's mark *G*. The top moulding is a modern addition. This rarity is said to have belonged to a Yorkshireman, William Bland; it was found in the possession of a family of farmers at Pateley Bridge, Nidderdale, Yorks, and was given by Canon Charles Robinson, D.D., sometime Master of St Catherine's College,

Illustrations

Cambridge, to the late Fred Roe, R.I. *Author's Collection.*

FIG. 10—Two oak chairs. *Left*: Yorkshire or Derbyshire 'Mortuary Chair', *circa* 1655, the back rails exhibiting small bearded masks said to symbolize King Charles I. *Photo by courtesy of S. W. Wolsey Ltd. Right*: Of slightly later period, a type which persisted to an advanced date in the century. Bought at Oxford in 1933 by the late Fred Roe, R.I. *Author's Collection.*

FIG. 11—Two chairs of the end of the seventeenth century. *Left*: Oak, from Weaverham, Cheshire. (*Photo by courtesy of 'The Connoisseur'*). *Right*: Stained Fruitwood, with caned back and seat (the front rail a later replacement), said to have come from a farmhouse in the Aylesbury area, and probably of Buckinghamshire make. *Both in the Author's Collection.*

FIG. 12—Rush-seated Elm Chairs of early eighteenth-century types. Note the unperforated splats in the backs; such chairs are often called 'fiddle-backs', though the design of the splat is based on that of a baluster or vase. These examples came from Gloucestershire, but similar chairs are often found elsewhere. *By courtesy of Mr Desmond Butler.*

FIG. 13—Eighteenth-century chairs of so-called 'Country Chippendale' types. *Left*: One of a small but heavy pair of oak, in style about mid-century but perhaps somewhat traditional. Note relatively simple piercing of the vase-splat. *Right*: Cherry-wood of good colour, and of a design frequently met with in the second half of the century. *Both in a private Collection.*

FIG. 14—Oak chairs of so-called 'Country Chippendale' design and of types fashionably made of mahogany, third quarter of the eighteenth century. Note how the vase-splat was by now elaborately perforated; and how, in country pieces, the traditional method of joining the front-rail to the legs was adhered to, instead of setting it back so as to link with the side-rails. *Both in the Author's Collection.*

FIG. 15—Contrasted chairs of the latter part of eighteenth century. *Left*: Rush-seated 'spindle-back' of a type which lingered, modified, into the nineteenth century. This example has a shaped top, a good front-rail, and tapered front legs with 'bun-feet'. *Author's Collection. Right*: So-called 'Country Chippendale' type; an obvious country piece which had found its way to London. *In a private Collection.*

FIG. 16—Some Windsor types. *Top left*: With shaped cresting, unperforated splat and cabriole front-legs, assigned to *circa* 1760-70, though perpetuating certain earlier characteristics. *By courtesy of M. Harris & Sons. Top right*: Simpler stick-back and -leg variety, eighteenth century, said to have come from Wales. *In Mr Peter Desborough's Collection. Bottom left*: Hoop-back chair, with 'Prince of Wales' Feathers' splat, *circa* 1800. *Belonging to Miss Frances Roe. Bottom right*: Nineteenth-century Armchair, showing a late form of back conforming with Victorian taste. *Author's Collection.*

FIG. 17—Chairs representing two of many lesser Windsor types, nineteenth century, perhaps both Wycombe-made. *Left*: 'Smoker's Bow,' with maker's stamp, DH in kidney-shaped compartment, on back-edge of seat. *Right*: Scroll-back Chair of common type, the back reflecting Regency characteristics. *Private Collection.*

FIG. 18—Ladder-back Chairs with rush-seats. *Left*: Elm and fruit-wood, eighteenth century, a widely distributed type, this example being from Kent. *Right*: Cherry-wood, early nineteenth century, a child's chair branded with initials ID on top rung of back, from Bedfordshire, though this again is of a type found in many parts. *By courtesy of Mr Desmond Butler.*

FIG. 19—Tudor interior, showing plain type of fixed bench. The scene is laid in a school-room, but similar conditions obtained in other country settings. From an illustration of the second half of the sixteenth century to *The Lyfe of Roberte the Devyll*, as aquatinted for I. Herbert's edition (1798). *Author's Collection.*

FIG. 20—Unusual 10-legged Form of oak, a 'Commonwealth' type of about the middle of the seventeenth century. From the neighbourhood of Guildford, Surrey. (The large dentils are probably additions). *Author's Collection.*

FIG. 21—Fireside Settle, with box-seat, and a doored compartment in the outer end which is angled to form a draught-stop. Early eighteenth century. (*Photo by courtesy of S. W. Wolsey Ltd.*)

FIG. 22—Small square Joined Stool with box-seat ('stoole with a lock') carved with initials KS, seventeenth century. *Victoria and Albert Museum* (*Photo Crown Copyright*).

FIG. 23—Two Foot-Stools of elm. *Below*: Sixteenth century, found at Rye, Sussex. *Above*: A modern imitation of a late Gothic piece, made of old, re-used oak. *Both in the Author's Collection.* (*Photo by courtesy of 'The Connoisseur'*).

FIG. 24—Long Table of oak, a yeoman piece of the early seventeenth century, from a farmhouse near Stratford-upon-Avon; painted by J. Seymour Lucas, R.A., in his picture *A 'Whip' for Van Tromp* (1883); (Collections: J. Seymour Lucas, R.A., Sydney Williams Lee, F.R.I.B.A. (1917), Mr and Mrs Fred Roe, Mr H. Pelham Lee). (*Photo by courtesy of 'The Connoisseur'*). *Author's Collection.*

FIG. 25—Oak Table, second quarter of seventeenth century, from the neighbourhood of Princes Risborough, Bucks, in the 'Hampden Country'. A piece of so-called 'Commonwealth' type. *In Mr Peter Desborough's Collection.*

SECOND GROUP OF PLATES BETWEEN PAGES 96 AND 97

FIG. 26—*The Faithful Steward*: a bed-sitting-room of the time of Henry VII, showing furniture of the period. Engraving from John Nelson's *History and Antiquities of . . . Islington* (3rd ed., 1829) after a painted glass roundel formerly at Ward's Place, Islington. *Print in the Author's Collection.*

FIG. 27—Oak Gate-leg Table of simple form and superficially of 'early' type, though belonging to about the end of the seventeenth century. Note the late character of the quasi-Gothic arching comparable with the shaped heads of panels on 'Queen Anne' furniture. *By courtesy of Mr Desmond Butler.*

FIG. 28—An eighteenth-century Flap-Table in oak, of a type usually made in more fashionable woods for the 'town' market. On each side, one of the legs can be moved forward to support the flap, and when out of use the table can be stored against a wall. Though differently constructed in various details, such tables served a similar purpose to the 'Gate-leg' (*cp.* Fig. 27) which by this time was old-fashioned. *Belonging to Miss Frances Roe.*

FIG. 29—Though furnished with tapered legs of a sort popular about the end of the eighteenth century, this writing-table retains traditional features. The drawer-front overlapping its opening, and the moulding of the table-top, would not have been inappropriate to a piece of somewhere around a century earlier; and, instead of being in the modish mahogany or satinwood, the table is made of serviceable oak. Of such was the 'utility furniture' of the period. *In Mr Peter Desborough's Collection.*

FIG. 30—Small Tripod-Table of country make, its form indicating an early nineteenth-century date. As often happens, the top (though old) has been re-set. Such tables represent a phase of taste reacting against the more elaborate tripods of the eighteenth century; an elaboration in any case beyond the scope of the average country-craftsman who favoured plainer types. *By courtesy of Mr Desmond Butler.*

FIG. 31—Though it has suffered interference (*e.g.* reduction of the upper stage), this oak buffet, first half of seventeenth century, sufficiently demonstrates a class of furniture approximating to the true Court Cupboard (as defined by Mr Symonds) and also to the much misunderstood term 'Livery Cupboard'. *Victoria and Albert Museum (Photo Crown Copyright).*

FIG. 32—Welsh *Tridarn*, inscribed WI: IH BVDD DRVGAROG YN OL DY ALLV 1689 (translatable as 'Be merciful according to thine ability', between ownership-initials and date). The general character of the piece bears out the date carved on the canopy, though the lower stages are strongly traditional, harking back to the first half of the seventeenth century. Note, however, the late form of the applied split-spindles on the centre-stage, and of the flat, unperforated balusters in the sides of the canopy. This *Tridarn* is known to have been at Voelas, Bettws-y-Coed, for at least 88 years. (Tridarn literally means 'three-piece'). In the Collection of Colonel J. W. Wynne Finch, of Voelas. (*By courtesy of the owner, and of the National Museum of Wales for the photograph*).

FIG. 33—An example of Welsh conservatism. Apart from the date on it, this might pass muster in England as an early eighteenth-century Press Cupboard or 'Court Cupboard' (showing how that article of furniture had developed). It is, however, a *Cupboard Deuddarn*, of bog-oak, dated 1769 in brass-headed nails and retaining one of the initials of its original owner Ioan (John) Daniel. The *Deuddarn* was the Welsh two-tiered cupboard, as opposed to the *Tridarn* or three-tiered. *From a drawing by J. R. Fawcett Thompson. (By courtesy of the artist, and of the editor of 'The Connoisseur').*

FIG. 34—Oak Food-Hutch, Eastern Counties, first half of seventeenth century. The panels are pierced for ventilation, and the top is built-up in desk-form. *Now in the Victoria and Albert Museum. Photo by courtesy of Phillips of Hitchin Ltd.*

Illustrations

by Richard Cole, Ipswich. The case is largely of mahogany, the sides of the 'waist' being of stained oak. A dial showing phases of the moon is in the arch, and the ball-finials, often of brass, are here of gilded wood. *A Family Piece in the Author's Collection*.

FIG. 51—American Hanging or Mantel Clock, containing the label of the 'E. N. Welch Mfg Co., Forestville, Conn., U.S.A.', nineteenth century. The movement is driven by internal weights and pendulum and strikes on a spiral gong; the lower panel of the door has coloured under-glass ornament of a beehive. Varying in detail, clocks of this type are found in many English cottage-homes. *By courtesy of Mr Desmond Butler*.

FIG. 52—Relics of old country life. *Left to Right*: Rushlight-holder of wrought iron, a rare type allied to Firedog-construction (*cp*. Fig. 53), first half of seventeenth century. Tigerware 'Greybeard' or 'Bellarmine', dated 1660. ('Greybeards,' though widely used in England, were very often German importations; dated examples are rare). Brass (copper-bottomed) Muller of shoe form (the lid missing), engraved with DH parted by an esquire's helmet, earlier part of nineteenth century. *Author's Collection*.

FIG. 53—One of a pair of iron Firedogs or 'Cob-irons', with spit-hooks, and tops usable as plate-warmers, etc., first half of seventeenth century. On it hangs a pair of steel Ember- or Brand-Tongs, eighteenth century, the tongs sometime at Lingfield Place, Surrey. *Author's Collection*.

FIG. 54—Brass Candlesticks: Some Types. *Left*: Late seventeenth-early eighteenth century. *Centre*: Late seventeenth century (a Dutch importation). *Right*: Early eighteenth century (from Winslow, Bucks). *Author's Collection*.

FIG. 55—Brass Candlesticks: More Types. *Left*: Early eighteenth century (one of a pair). *Centre: circa* 1790-1800. *Right*: About the middle of eighteenth century (with adjustable socket in stem). *Author's Collection*.

FIG. 56—Stained-glass Quarries such as this were not limited to secular use, nor even to large mansions, but were sometimes found in the windows of smaller houses. This seventeenth-century quarry, with a shield of Seckford *impaling* Rowe or Roe, is said, however, to have come from old Intwood Hall, near Norwich. Since rebuilt, Intwood Hall had belonged to the Founder of the Royal Exchange, Sir Thomas Gresham; he was a cousin by marriage of Sir Thomas Rowe, Lord Mayor of London in 1568, one of whose granddaughters married into the Seckford family. *Author's Collection*. (*Photo by arrangement with the Editor of* '*Antiques*').

ILLUSTRATIONS IN THE TEXT

1 · Of Town and Country

FIRST, let us form a clear notion of what is really meant by 'country' furniture. In collectors' parlance, the term is rather loosely applied to pieces of a roughish sort or made of woods other than those in vogue in politer circles at the period of their construction. Not infrequently such pieces show traditional tendencies: the perpetuation of styles or ornament long since discarded by the more modish craftsmen. Within a little, the description of these as country furniture is often justified, though we may permit ourselves to examine the matter in closer detail.

Broadly speaking, the vogue at any given period was established in the larger towns and cities, whence it radiated outwards to rural districts where it may not have gained a hold until a later date. For this reason, 'town' furniture—that is furniture obviously conforming to the latest standards or the height of fashion, and produced with every refinement of the craftsmen's skill—may be easier to date closely than some bucolic survival fashioned more or less in the tradition of its maker's granfer. Once, having occasion to hang a good seventeenth-century panelled door in my country home, I found that circumstances required the addition of a closing-ring. A young local craftsman, whom I had employed for the job, took a look at the ancient fittings and, without further prompting from me, forged an iron ring and plate which, without imitation, harmonized with them far better than I had dared to expect. It is precisely this hang-over of country methods from one generation to another that perplexes inexperienced collectors. Time and again, I have been told of promising 'Gothic' chests which, on investigation, have turned out to be no earlier than seventeenth-century. Anything medieval in their appearance was solely due to their makers' retention of methods long since obsolete in town circles, or, at the best, relegated to pieces of the cheaper sort. It is no exaggeration to add that the humbler chests of late sixteenth- or seventeenth-century date sometimes exhibit features referable to even as far back as the thirteenth century. True, those features are extremely modified, but their mere presence is enough to testify to the profound continuity of the old English country life. The clash of the Roses and the Civil War, the upheaval of the Reformation, the impact of the Renaissance, had all but passed those methods by.

To my way of thinking, this is one of the reasons why country furniture is so attractive, telling, as it does, of something all but changeless and immutable: the unhurried heart of England.

Not that all country furniture is as leisurely in growth as this. There are pieces nearer the prevailing mode of the towns, distinguished, maybe, from it by pleasing individualisms. Such pieces—useful and agreeable things—are close enough to fashion to encourage the use of such terms as 'Country Chippendale': a label with no historic warranty to back it. The great Thomas Chippendale (1718-79) and his firm were but one among many notable craftsmen; nor is there the slightest reason to suppose that he was responsible for more than a fraction of the furniture now going under his name. 'Country Chippendale' simply means a class of country furniture alignable with more modish types of the sort popularly described as 'Chippendale'. It does not mean that such country furniture was made by Chippendale himself. Any 'country' label of this description should be regarded with reserve. Even in the big towns, the stars of furniture-making were attended by a host of lesser lights: craftsmen who reproduced the current styles in cheaper materials or in simpler forms adapted to the needs of humbler folk. Thus, though some furniture is plainly of rustic origin, there are other pieces (also known as 'country') of which the origin is less obvious.

A point to be borne in mind is that, in the past, town and country lay nearer together than they do to-day. In the case of London, the long sprawl of the suburbs had not yet come into being. Islington, for instance, is now very much a part of London. In George III's time, it was still remote enough for pedestrians to gather at the *Angel*, so as to cross the fields in company and thus frustrate the footpads. A relative of my mother's—a relative who died in 1833—was eased of a valuable watch in that same waste between Islington and London. Kensington, despite its Royal Palace, was still a country village; and between Chelsea and the village of Brompton stretched the furze-covered Chelsea Common, where Parliament troops had mustered in the Civil War. Even in my father's younger days, a part of Chelsea Common (bordering Thistle Grove) still survived in the form of market gardens. Thomas Henry Huxley tells us that, when he was born at Ealing on a May morning in 1825, that now so populous suburb was 'as quiet a little country village as could be found within half-a-dozen miles of Hyde Park Corner.'[1]

With such examples in view—and they could be easily multiplied—it is clear enough that the country pressed much more closely on the town than it does to-day. The young George Morland, living in Windmill Street, off Tottenham Court Road, had only to go out of doors to see the mill itself; at Hampstead or with the Wards at Kensal Green he was in the very country. The town gave out at the public-house by Whitefield's Chapel in the Tottenham Court Road, and it is quite on the cards that some of Morland's most rural scenes were laid in spots now well within the urban area. To quote C. Reginald Grundy: 'In those days the inhabitants of the outlying London suburbs were virtually in the country. Pleasant little woodland glades were almost at their doors, and children might not only be seen playing in them, but might be easily enticed indoors to "sit" as models.'[2]

With this and similar instances in view, we can freely appreciate how falsely based is any attempt too strictly to separate town and country furniture. 'Town' was no more exclusively the province of aristocrats or wealthy burgesses, than 'country' was the sole preserve of the peasantry or the farming interest. In both were rich and poor, squire and hind. Townsfolk of the humbler grades had neither the means nor the inclination to buy chairs of Mr Chippendale, nor, for that matter, from Messrs Vile and Cobb, nor Messrs Ince and Mayhew, nor Mr Manwaring. They had no truck with the firm of Hepplewhite nor the chaste designs of Mr Sheraton. They went and bought a good, honest-to-God chair made for hard usage at the cost of a few shillings; and if that chair happened to reflect the taste of Mr Chippendale or other great men, so much the better. Quite likely, they went in for a Windsor chair of one of the sorts we shall meet in detail later—including those Mr Morland certainly knew, however carelessly he drew them. And whether that 'Windsor' was made somewhere around High Wycombe, or in Norfolk or Suffolk, or what-have-you? it was all-the-same 'Windsor' when it was not 'Dan Day'. In London alone there must have been a quite considerable proportion of furniture which, wherever it was actually produced, would now qualify as 'country'.

Your fine gentleman might grace his *salons* with new suites in (let us say) the exquisite Adam taste. His side-tables and commodes might bear the elegant if somewhat spineless, classical fancies

[1] For *Notes* see end of book.

associated with the brushes of Mrs Angelica Kauffman or Mr Cipriani; but there was no particular reason why the servants' quarters should be similarly dignified. For such as these, good, honest furniture of the lesser grades was normally sufficient: furniture of types now sometimes freely classed as country-made. In addition, there might also be still usable waifs from older times: out-moded furniture of bygone styles and fashions now regarded as being too barbarous for the delectation of the *monde*.

One speaks here of town usage, but, relatively, much the same applied to the more fashionable country mansions, and, indeed, to others less concerned with the vogue of the moment. However strong was our ancestors' sense of tradition, it is plain enough that, on the whole, the cult of antiquities as such made but small appeal to them. Of course, there were enthusiasts like 'Horry' Walpole or the somewhat eccentric Sir John Soane; but even these were beset by romantic whimsies foreign to our present scientific attitude towards the study of antiques. Naturally, one cannot ignore the more intimate appeal of such matters as family relics (where these were respected). As illustrating this: my good friend Peter Desborough, representative of a cadet branch of the stock which bore Noll's brother-in-law, Major-General John Disbrowe, wistfully eyes a certain footnote in Noble's *Memoirs of the Protectoral-House of Cromwell* (I quote from the 2nd edition, 1787, Vol. II, p.295 *n*): 'A friend of mine says, the mansion at Trimnalls [in the parish of Downham, Essex, an estate purchased by the Major-General's 7th son, Benjamin,] was large, surrounding a court; and where he has seen the major-general's buffcoat, and hat of the same materials, lined with an iron plate, with the furniture he left behind him, . . .' Admittedly this was a Great House, but similar motives of affection caused many an item of family interest to be preserved in much humbler homes. All the same, it may be said that, within a little, the current skilled appreciation of old English furniture is a modern growth, comprised well within the last hundred years.

Frequently one finds an old country-house which, at this period or that, has been brought up-to-date in its equipment. Time may have stood still for it since then, but perhaps in the time of Elizabeth, perhaps in that of Charles II, perhaps much later, all the principal rooms were renovated and their ancient furniture banished to limbo.

In my own family, in the then still countrified county town of

Ipswich, there occurred an instance of a process that had been going on all over England throughout the ages. 'I can myself remember as a boy,' so wrote my father in his *Old Oak Furniture*,[3] 'that, in a home where mahogany and horsehair were plentiful, the finest piece of furniture in the whole house was abandoned to the housekeeper's room, as an out-of-date thing and of no particular interest. The piece in question happened to be a superb English buffet, inlaid with ivory and mother-of-pearl, bearing the date 1661 on its front.' Fortunately, this admirable piece was not only in first-rate condition but was kept in such by the attentions of the housekeeper, who had a special liking for it. It thus 'received more care and attention than the rest of the household's belongings', and as I remember it a finer example of its kind and period could not be desired.

I should have liked to have had the looting of that housekeeper's room. The 1661 'buffet', alas! has long since gone elsewhere; but from that same room came a good plain mahogany bureau-bookcase of the latter part of the eighteenth century. This, affectionately known as 'Uncle Owen's bookcase', is in my study to-day, where visitors always eye it admiringly.

Now the point of all this is that Uncle Owen—more precisely he was my grand-uncle Owen Roe of Museum Street, Ipswich, who died in 1884, aged 87—was a keen collector and an able connoisseur. A great Rembrandt, *An Evangelist writing*, now in the Boymans Museum at Rotterdam, and sometime in the collections of Sir Joshua Reynolds, Charles M. Schwab and Lord Duveen of Millbank, hung in his drawing-room. He very probably owned that famous Gainsborough, now in the National Gallery, of *The Painter's Daughters Chasing a Butterfly*. His collection included the work of men like Crome and Etty. The stand he used to hold his music when he was minded to play the violin is beside me at this moment. But when it came to a really excellent piece of furniture of the year following that of the Glorious Restoration, he put it away 'for use' in the housekeeper's room. Nothing could more aptly illustrate the change of sentiment in regard to antique furniture that has come about within a relatively short space of time.

I do not suggest for one moment that this splendid waif from Charles II's reign was anything but a town piece, but it carries us on to another point of consequence. It is not to be supposed that furniture found in the country was necessarily country-made. Nowadays, the movement of antiquities from one district to another, by the ordinary process of trading, has reached such proportions that many a piece of furniture may have come from almost anywhere. It may have been through a London saleroom before it reached the picturesque little shop where you first set eyes on it. If you buy an old Windsor chair in or around High Wycombe—well, it may have been made in that district so long associated with the production of 'Windsors'; but whether it has been all along in that locality is, perhaps, another matter. There are, of course, cases in which one can be certain—or reasonably so—that furniture has never been more than the proverbial stone's-throw from the place of its discovery, though the chances of finding such pieces are greatly decreased, and the scientific study of local types is correspondingly hindered and complicated. No longer is there much chance of discovering Elizabethan (or at any rate seventeenth-century) panelling in a pig-sty (as a certain clergyman once did in Suffolk), or of 'digging out' really fine furniture from lofts and barns. Yet such lucky strikes have been made in the past, when furniture collectors were few and ploughed an all-but-virgin field.

As an instance of the fate of furniture which had fallen out of favour, my father—a pioneer of the study of old oak—drew attention, many years ago, to a detail in a painting by David Teniers the younger (1610-1690), in the National Gallery, London. It is the picture known as *An Old Woman peeling a pear*, once owned by the 'burlesque Napoleon', Jerome Bonaparte, and as the background was used more than once by Teniers, it is safe to assume that it was based on some spot known to him.

The scene is laid in one of those ancient barns, the incidental uses of which are demonstrated in old Dutch paintings by the presence of boors carousing, or the usual dirty old man tumbling the usual witless wench. In the present case, an honest elderly body pauses from peeling fruit to glance at the spectator. What really concerns us now, however, is that dimly in the background can be seen a wainscot chair, and a credence-cupboard of late Gothic form—a piece which nowadays would grace any of the more princely collections of old oak furniture.

Clearly here was a piece once modish, but which had become so hopelessly old-fashioned that it had sunk to such menial purposes as holding the shepherd's raddle or the miscellaneous lumber of the hinds. Nobody wanted it, but it was just too good to be broken up for kindling. Maybe it has long since come to such an end; but should it have survived some centuries of neglect, its original owner's taste would have been more than justified. This, it is true, is a Dutch example, but what is true of the seventeenth-century Netherlands is no less true of rural England as concerns the general disregard of antique furniture. Pieces discarded from the Great House might enter the cottage or the barn; they might even be bought by the tenantry from motives of affection when an old estate was sold up. (Contrary to modern propaganda, there was often a real affection and a mutual interdependence between Hall and hamlet.) But whether such once superior pieces were what is really meant by 'country' furniture is a point only to be decided from internal evidence and such scraps of pedigree as may have survived the tooth of time.

2 · Of Old Country Homes

ONE could not omit all mention of the Great House; but, having mentioned it, let us buckle closely to our theme. Our principal concern is with the smaller house, the farmhouse—and the cottage, and, still more precisely, with their furniture. Having grasped the difficulties attendant on a recognition of country types, let us next consider what of them we are likely to find in an old-world setting of the kinds envisaged.

Anyone who has ever lived, or been, in a cottage will readily understand that its resources are limited. Obviously not more than a small proportion of the items discussed in this book are likely to be found there. Assuming (as we doubtless may) that the most crowded hour of cottage-life was in the later Victorian and Edwardian periods, it is at least probable that even ancient cottages are now not only more furnished, but perhaps sometimes better furnished, than they were in their prime. I am not here following to its logical extremity Mr Osbert Lancaster's diverting comparison of the 'traditional' and the 'cultured' cottage, though doubtless the impact of the cultured carpet-bagger on the countryside has had a salutary effect in helping to dispel the clutter of ugly nonsense without which no cottage-home was once felt to be tolerable. The tendency to over-furnish and to crowd with knick-knacks, so characteristic of later Victorian town-life, was reflected in the homes of country-dwellers, where its tastelessness was even harder to avoid. Where once the peasantry was content with crude but spirited figures of the pottery of Staffordshire, or brass candlesticks of good, but simple, form, there developed an eruption of imitation-lace curtains, with aspidistras in 'art' pots, masses of self-conscious photographs in hideous frames, and revolting little images of boys and girls with lacey frills that all too readily chipped and broke away. With such as these, and their attendant varnished and plush-seated furniture—'our saddle-bag suite which defies competition', as Barry Pain once put it—this book has no concern. Such things may be on the way to becoming antiques, though, for the sake of our credit with posterity, one could wish that they would not arrive. We may poke fun at the 'cultured cottage' and its preciosity, but it has helped to bring a new simplicity to country life.

That simplicity is subtly different from the old. Your bygone cottager, as indeed your modern cottager of the true breed, had few ideas on the art of spacing things for effect's sake. Any art he had was largely intuitive. What he was mainly concerned with was utility, and if his home was sparsely furnished it was because of lack of means and space. One has merely to study the arrangement of the doors in many ancient cottages to realize how impossible it would have been to find sufficient wall-space to accommodate bulky furniture. Yet even relatively bulky pieces somehow found their way into the least likely of those low-ceilinged rooms. If a large press—perhaps contemptuously discarded from the Great House—could not go against a wall, it might be used as a sort of partition to divide the available space. All the same, your medieval cottager, as well as he of sundry later periods, was probably content with little in the way of furniture. A chest or so, a bed of sorts (quite likely made up on the floor), some stools, a rough table (if no other piece would serve) and possibly a hutch for food would be about as much as an average cottage could be expected to contain; apart, that is, from such things as crocks and skillets and a spoon or two (of wood, say, or base metal), an iron pot on its hake over the fire, and maybe fire-dogs, with a rush-jack or some other primitive form of lighting—such would be the principal equipment of the home, as distinct from implements of the field or the cottar's craft or trade. When William Cobbett wrote in his *Rural Rides* (1830; p.242) of the farmer's provision for his labourers of 'a kitchen for them to sit in, bed rooms for them to sleep in, tables, and stools, and benches of everlasting duration', he was recording a long-existent state of affairs.

These words of the redoubtable Cobbett's were occasioned by his visit to a farm-sale near Hartswood in Surrey on 20th October 1825. Prettily situated by the River Mole, the farm in question had been occupied for a great number of years by a family named Charington. 'Everything about this farm-house,' wrote Cobbett in *Rural Rides* (p.241), 'was formerly the scene of *plain manners* and *plentiful living*. Oak clothes-chests, oak bedsteads, oak chests of drawers, and oak tables to eat on, long, strong, and well supplied with joint stools. Some of the things were many hundreds of years old. But all appeared to be in a state of decay and nearly of disuse.'

What galled Cobbett's sense of the fitness of things was that this neglect of good, sound, usable stuff had been accompanied, even encouraged, by an attempt to ape town fashions. The ancestral oak might fall into decay, but, says Cobbett contemptuously, there was a *parlour*. And in that parlour were 'the mahogany table, and the fine chairs, and the fine glass, and all as bare-faced upstart as any stock-jobber in the kingdom can boast of.'

Cobbett was not to know that the very things at which he grumbled would themselves doubtless graduate as desirable antiques; but in essence his complaint was sound enough. Instead of minding his own affairs, the farmer was aping the town gentleman's setting and going broke in the process. It was the same false notion of up-to-dateness and a pseudo-respectability that was later to encourage small householders (some of whom could not play a note) to equip themselves with two or three extremely shiny pianos. In other words, it was just so much snobbery: a snobbery which must have had a considerable effect in ousting the true country furniture in favour of town products—or their imitations.

To realize how pleasant a place a true farmhouse kitchen could be in the late eighteenth - early nineteenth century, we have only to turn to Rowlandson's drawing (Fig. 1) of *Dr. Syntax turned Nurse*, aquatinted in 1820 as one of the plates for *The Third Tour of Dr. Syntax*. Hams are hooked to the ceiling-beams (as in Mr. Pickwick's day they were at Dingley Dell), a fixed dresser is garnished with plates, dishes, and a harvester's keg for taking out drink to the fields. There are ladder-back chairs, a bureau for the goodman's whiplashes and papers of account, a hooded cradle of basket-work on wooden rockers. A warming-pan hangs by the door, a round-faced clock with pendulum-case ticks over the fireplace; spice-cupboard and salt-box have their places nearby. As was remarked in my *Rowlandson* (1947), doubtless all the wooden furniture was made of oak, elm, beech or other varieties at the time unmodish, but the place is sightly and liveable. Quite likely Rowlandson based his drawing on some kitchen actually seen by him on one or other of his sketching trips. Its homely comfort and its broad-beamed hostess (in imminent need of another cradle) were just the sort of thing he had an eye to—not excepting the slimmer, more bedworthy lass he glimpsed through a door washing clothes in the background.

It is not within the scope of this book to encompass a closely documented survey of the diversities of furnishing in a series of periods. Such, though valuable to the antiquary and the student of manners, might well become tedious to the reader whose need is more general. Yet there may well be point in discussing at this stage the contents of one of the smaller country-houses at the time of the Commonwealth, as disclosed by its owner's last will and testament. I have selected this will for two reasons: firstly, because it represents a way of life that was not only long-established but, *mutatis mutandis*, was to endure for generations; secondly, because in my insistence on the relative paucity of furniture in the cottage, I must not seem to imply that 'smaller' homes above the cottage class were no more lavishly equipped. It is, for example, well known that the prosperity of the latter part of the sixteenth century reacted very favourably on the condition of farmers—and not only farmers on a large scale. William Harrison (1534-1593), whose *Description of England* (1577) gives a very different picture from that in Cobbett's *Rural Rides* two hundred and fifty years later, tells us that 'manie farmers, . . . by vertue of their old and not of their new leases have for the most part learned also to garnish their cupbords with plate.' And in a famous passage he tells us that a farmer would 'thinke his gaines verie small towards the end of his terme, if he have not six or seven yeares rent lieing by him, beside a fair garnish of pewter on his cupbord, with so much more in od vessels going about the house, three or foure feather beds, so many coverlids and carpets of tapestrie, a silver salt, a bowle for wine, and a dozen spoones to furnish up the sute.' When Harrison spoke of a 'fair garnish' he meant a seemly one, the word 'fair' not having then acquired its modern popular connotation of 'moderate'.

Harrison's is an attractive pen-picture, showing us how wrong it is for modern upstarts to despise a good yeoman descent. Unfortunately it reveals a way of life which was doomed to decay, though its traces long lingered. We can still detect signs of it in the Commonwealth will to which allusion has already been made and to which we now come. It was made on 12th July 1650, and proved on 11th March 1656 (1657 New Style).[4] It was drawn for one of a family (distantly related to mine) living at the village of Debach in Suffolk: a family of yeoman rank though this member of it made his will as 'gent'. He was baptized at Debach on 19th March 1621-22, and was buried there on 25th December in 1656, having had by his wife Elizabeth a son and namesake, born at Debach on 29th November 1646.

Our testator's finances were not in good heart; he owed money and there were mortgages to be met; but when we arrive at that part of the will relating to his household effects, we see that, debts or no debts, this gentleman-farmer had enjoyed comfortable surroundings. To his 'loveing wife Elizabeth', he bequeathed 'one posted bedstead and settle', with mattress, curtains and valance, featherbed, bolster and two pillows, two blankets and a coverlet. Next come two interesting items, 'one paire of Iron copirons with brasse', these being what we should now term fire-dogs or andirons of mixed metals; and 'one stoole with a lock', evidently a joined stool with a box seat and lifting top forming its lid (*cp.* Fig. 22). These again are followed by 'one greate box', the ensuing words 'as they are nowe standing in the Parlour' presumably relating to all the preceding items, which in view of our ancestors' taste for bed-sitting rooms is not as strange as might otherwise appear, especially in view of the fact that the testator was 'sicke and weake' when his will was drawn. Not but what this particular bequest can be paralleled in other documents. Have we not the allusion to 'twoe joyned beddes in my parlor' in the sufficiently well-known will (1581) of Richard Hathaway of Shottery, father-in-law (as is generally accepted) of William Shakespeare? In those days, 'parlour' was a less restricted term than it has since become. Also to his 'loveing wife', our Suffolk testator of 1650 bequeathed one 'wenscot [wainscot] chest in the parlour chamber', and a quantity of specified linen—one notes in passing a tablecloth and towels; pewter—10 dishes, 2 salt-cellars, 3 porringers, 2 candlesticks; a brass kettle, pot, and skillet, and sundry other matters.

His silver was left to his son—2 cups and 6 spoons 'to bee kept for him by my loveing wife till he come of the age of one and twenty yeares'. The other provisions of the will do not concern the theme of this book, but enough indication of the equipment of that Suffolk home has been given to set any antiquary's mouth awatering. Here was no fine gentleman, but a substantial yeoman-farmer with property in more than one parish: a yeoman in debt, but none the less comfortably housed, and with comely household goods at his command.

Your cottar (to return to him) did not live in even so relatively modest a style, nor would he have had much chance of gleaning exalted ideas on furnishing from his periodic visits to the smaller class of 'local'. One is not speaking so much of the great coaching-inns (though even in those the method of furnishing might be inferior) as of the village ale-houses where the equipment of the public rooms was often of the simplest. Admittedly there are some rather notable exceptions to this generalization—one cannot forget that a magnificent linen-fold settle-back, now in the Victoria and Albert Museum, was within living memory in the *Green Dragon* at Combe St. Nicholas, Somerset; but even nowadays one can still find pleasant country inns where such innovations as bar-counters[5] are still to seek: inns, where one takes one's ease on benches fixed to the walls behind well-scoured tables, and where one's drink is drawn by hand, cool from the cellar on a sultry day. In the past, such houses of call were numerous, and even when their furniture was less primitive, it seldom reached a lofty standard, and then sometimes by the chance acquisition of outmoded waifs which had known better days.

Among the less reputable boozing-kens in town and country alike were many such as appear in a little oil painting on copper now before me. It is a shoddy, though not unclever, little work of a sort that would not have been amiss in the uncritical atmosphere of one of the smaller country-homes about 1790. Its painter thought well enough of it to place his HB monogram on the top of the upturned cask that served the topers for a table. HB's identity is unknown to me—not that it matters much. His technique is akin to that of the paintings on the lids of the less excellent circular boxes and other products of the 'toy trade' at Birmingham and elsewhere: paintings not infrequently based, at sundry removes, on works by old masters.

Such has happened in this case. Were the pedigree of HB's composition to be fully explored, it would hark back, through various intermediary stages, to the carousal scenes so prevalent in Dutch painting of the seventeenth century, though a decided attempt has been made to bring the dress of the figures up-to-date—especially in the case of the fuddled personage, resembling a seedy edition of Charles James Fox, on the right of the picture.

The scene depicts two rogues engaged in the lucrative process of 'plucking a pigeon'. They are drinking in a beamed room, with a printed broadside pinned to one of its walls; and the victim's chair is of the plainest stick-back sort procurable. There is no comfort, save that of a roof, a seat, and liquor, of which there was doubtless a copious supply, not improbably hocussed. It was in such dens as this that a deal of the recreational side of low life was enjoyed.

Beyond the remains of a modern label showing that the painting was at one time in an ownership near High Wycombe, there is no indication of its history; but, indifferent though it be, the little work is not without its interest as a comment on manners in a period not vastly remote from our own.

3 . Of Chests and Coffers

WHETHER in Town or Country, the class of furniture taking premier place by ancient right and custom is undoubtedly the Chest. Even the humblest chest can claim a pedigree far longer than any king's. One can, of course, assume that so essential a thing as a four-sided container plus lid and bottom could originate independently in widely separated lands: but the fact remains that of all furniture it yields to none in ancientry. Indeed, it has its place in the Osirian legend of Ancient Egypt, though, as our business is solely with the English rural scene, we need not linger on its international background.

For one thing, it was a piece of many uses. It would hold your clothes, or valuables, or those papers which, not improbably, your man-of-law could read much better than you could hope to do. It would serve as seat, table, dresser, or even bedstead in appropriate cases. These are commonplaces; but anyone who has lived with chests as much as I have done knows them to be literally true. In the issue of *Eve, The Lady's Pictorial*, for 26th October 1921, there was reproduced an interesting photograph of the kitchen of 'an old farmhouse in Oxfordshire dated 1662'. It shows a fixed dresser, and a table and form, all of rough construction; but, what is to our present purpose, in the inglenook by the open-hearth fire stands a much used boarded chest at least as old as the seventeenth century, and still serving the dual function of a receptacle and a fireside seat. Beyond all question, the chest was, *par excellence*, the prime essential of the home-life of our earlier ancestors.

Boarded chest? That needs explanation.

For our purpose, medieval chests may be defined as approximating to one of three related types: the 'dug-out,' the 'boarded,' and the 'framed'. Of these, the 'dug-out' or 'trunk'—the latter a term which has come down to us from days when a tree-trunk was actually used for the purpose—is the most primitive, consisting of a block of timber with a receptacle gouged out of the solid and fitted with a lid. Surviving examples of this elementary form of construction are commonly referred to a remote period, and in some few cases not without probability, though others may actually have been made a good deal later than at first sight appears. A moment's reflection will show that, especially in backward communities, primitive methods of construction may persist without material modification for a very long while. Indeed, almost the sole clue to the age of many dug-outs lies in certain details of their ironwork. This is scarcely a matter to be pursued in the present book, as dug-out chests of any sort very seldom occur on the market.

Old travelling trunks of interest, however, do sometimes turn up, their rounded lids dimly recalling the distant days when the shape was actually dictated by the curve of the tree. One such trunk, constructed of thin timber, varnished or stained on the outside, came to light in the neighbourhood of the village of Speen, near Princes Risborough, while this book was being written (Fig. 4). It is furnished with three drawers, side-by-side, in the lower part, and the exterior is ornamented with brass-headed nails, some ornamentally disposed and others (on the lid) forming the legend E H 1685. I am given to understand by Mr Desmond Butler, who discovered the trunk, that there are grounds for thinking that E H may have been a member of a family named Harmon—with Harman and Hermon a locally-found name; but the most interesting thing about the trunk is that it is almost completely lined with contemporary paper, block-printed with figure subjects, some of them showing the dress of the period (Fig. 4). This noteworthy piece, which at one time rested on two much decayed joined stools, was used by its former owner as a clothes-chest.

A still more curious example, dated 1649 in brass-headed nails, was given to the Victoria and Albert Museum by Colonel Henry Howard, F.S.A. It is of leather-covered wood lined with canvas, and has in its top a conical projection to accommodate the tall steeple-hat as worn about the time of King Charles' execution. This trunk belonged to Edward Bushell (1604-1671) of Cleeve Prior Manor House, Worcestershire, and 'was hidden away in a dark attic' there when Colonel Howard 'purchased it from the owners of the property in 1922.'[6] Dimly related to such things as the 'Harmon' trunk are the hair-trunks of various sizes and generally of much later date, at one time favoured for travelling purposes; but enough for our purpose has been said about trunks.

We are thus left with the 'boarded' and 'framed' types of chest; the latter being a complex refinement of the simpler form. It will become obvious why the distinction is insisted on, though 'small collectors' are warned that their chances of obtaining true medieval examples of either are practically *nil*. Almost all the surviving specimens belong to cathedrals, parish churches, or ancient institutions linked with the Church, though a few have escaped to museums or influential private collections. And whether or not church chests were town- or country-made, they clearly lie outside the collector's proper province, save in so far as they afford evidence or provide examples for comparative study. In fact it would seem that at any rate many of the less spectacular examples were probably of more or less local origin, though evidence exists to suggest the presence of certain centres of distribution. Such was doubtless the case with the so-called Kentish-Gothic coffers at Faversham, Rainham, and St. John's Hospital, Canterbury—all in the Garden of England—which may well have emanated from one and the same workshop—that of a fourteenth-century craftsman of considerable ability. For the reason already cited, allusions to church furniture in these pages are necessarily few, though the collector in search of comparative examples should bear in mind its value as a means of reference. With certain rather obvious exceptions, there is no reason to believe that the majority of church chests differed materially from those in secular use, though the more bulky or elaborate of them would have been in no wise suited to the average small dwelling.

The boarded chest (Fig. 2) originated from the heavily built receptacles in use before the introduction of the framed variety, though it must not be assumed that the one type was immediately superseded by the other. Broadly speaking, the earlier of these types was that in which the face was formed of large wooden planks disposed to present a relatively flush surface. Such chests, often heavily guarded with iron work, presented a front extending unbroken to its junction with the ends, and it is from such pieces that the more lightly constructed boarded chests of later times are descended.

In the thirteenth century, however, a strong but simple method of framing became popular. In this type, the front, though still flush (or nearly so), was enclosed by stiles or uprights often of great breadth, while the ends might be stoutly coffered.[7] From this to the framed chest of later times was but a step, but that the step was not immediate is shown by such an item as the superb fourteenth-century chest in Huttoft Church, Lincolnshire. This, though it has a superficial appearance of being panelled, is actually constructed on

Notes on Plates, see P. 12

1 *Dr. Syntax turned Nurse*, by Thomas Rowlandson

2 *Top:* Small boarded chest, *c.* 1500 **3** *Foot:* Framed plain chest, seventeenth century

4 Travelling trunk, dated 1685, and (*below*) its block-printed lining paper

5 Framed chest, dated [16]95

6 So-called ‘ Bible-boxes ’; (*top*) sixteenth century ; (*centre*) dated 1652 **7** *Foot :* Table desk or ‘ desk-box ’, dated 1682

8 *Left* : Club tobacco-box, early eighteenth century, and a seventeenth-century joined stool **9** *Right* : 'William Bland's chair'

10 *Top :* ' Mortuary ' chair, and another chair of about the middle of the seventeenth century **11** *Foot :* Late seventeenth-century chairs

12 *Top :* Early eighteenth-century chairs **13** *Foot :* So-called ' Country Chippendale ' chairs

14 *Top :* More so-called ' Country Chippendale ' chairs **15** *Foot :* Eighteenth-century spindle-back chair, and a ' Country Chippendale' chair

16 Types of Windsor chairs from George III to Queen Victoria

17 *Top* : Late types of Windsor chairs **18** *Foot* : Ladder-back chairs, eighteenth and early nineteenth century

19 Tudor interior, showing plain fixed bench

20 *Top* : Ten-legged form of ' Commonwealth ' type **21** *Foot* : Fireside settle, early eighteenth century

22 *Left* : Square joined stool with box-seat, seventeenth century **23** *Right* : Foot-stools ; (*below*) sixteenth century ; (*above*) a modern imitation

24 Long table, early seventeenth century, found at Stratford-upon-Avon

25 Table, second quarter of seventeenth century

the old plank (boarded) principle, though with applied tracery and buttresses.[8] Indeed, though the framed chest was to achieve a popularity that all but ousted the boarded variety from polite usage—there are certain exceptions, as in the case of 'Nonsuch' and 'poker-work' chests of the later sixteenth and the seventeenth centuries—both boarded and framed types continued to be made, though many of the later boarded chests are suggestive of a country origin.

It is from the early framed chest that was developed the panelled chest with its complex structure of panels and framework (Figs. 3. and 5). This does not mean that all panelled chests are of superior quality. As with other types of furniture, they belong to every grade from the aristocratic to the humble; and, as a convenient rule-of-thumb, it can be accepted that, on the whole, the more splendid and refined its execution, the more likely it is that a given chest is a town piece. But, as already indicated, it is often difficult, if not impossible, to draw a strict dividing line as between, say, the good work of a superior country craftsman and the indifferent performance of an inferior worker in one of the more populous centres.

The essential conservatism of the boarded type of chest is demonstrated not only in its persistent adherence to an ancient form of construction, but, maybe, in the ornament incised or carved on it. Whorls or roundels of a sort descended at long last from those on thirteenth-century furniture are sometimes found on chests of seventeenth-century date, placed there, perhaps, because the rural craftsman had seen something of the sort in his parish church and instinctively adapted it to his own purposes. When it becomes accessible to collectors, the boarded chest has reached the form which, with minor modifications, it retained from the latter part of the fifteenth century to a very much later period. That is to say, front, back and sides each present a flush surface, the ends being formed of single planks prolonged to form supports. In certain examples, the supports show a forward 'kick' at the front of the footing, the projection being sometimes fashioned like a small buttress of Gothic character (Fig. 2), though in later times this Gothicness was lost. Also, the end-elevation is frequently terminated at the base by an angular excision which in some of the earlier examples is shaped like a debased Gothic arch-head. Arching of the lower edge of the front is also found in certain, usually early, examples. In this case, 'early' is a relative term, applied to chests of *circa* 1500 or rather later, though it should be made clear that well-formed buttress-feet have been noticed on chests of considerably later period than this. Indeed, collectors will do well to avoid a too optimistic dating of the boarded chests with which we are now dealing. There is a common tendency to ante-date examples which merely perpetuate traditional methods. A boarded chest of 'late Gothic' times usually declares itself by unmistakeable allusions to its period.* By far the greater number of boarded chests that reach the market are of seventeenth-century date; in some cases, even later. Now and again, it is still possible to detect local tendencies in carving. In *The Connoisseur* (June 1948), Mr Symonds (discussing *The Regional Design & Ornament of Joined Furniture*) interestingly demonstrated the existence of what may be tentatively called a Northamptonshire School of sixteenth- and seventeenth-century boarded chests, one of its characteristics being a distinctively rendered 'trail' of undulating leafage, though, as he truly pointed out, trails are also found in various other parts of England. They are, indeed, a 'hang-over' from the Gothic, though often differing in detail from the medieval idiom.

Of framed or (as we may now call them) panelled chests, it is scarcely necessary to say much in this place. Examples of a date earlier than the reign of Elizabeth are so difficult to obtain as to be almost out of the reckoning. The most prevalent type is that with panels carved with the linenfold, a motif which, though clearly medieval in idea, does not appear until the close of the Middle Ages (Fig. 47). A vague suggestion to the effect that it was used on linen-chests is thrown right out of court by the mere fact that the same motif is found on panelling, chairs, and other furniture which could not possibly be so used. Nobody believes that story nowadays; it is merely mentioned here as a sample of the nonsense that gets talked by those whose knowledge of antiquities and the ways of artist-craftsmen is inadequate. To understand medieval ornament, one has first to appreciate that whereas some motifs are symbolical or directly representational, others were occasioned simply by their suitability or because they happened to please. There is no use trying to discover a recondite significance where none existed. A good deal has been surmised about the incidence of linenfold. There is a doubtful though gracious theory that it was suggested by the Veil of the Chalice; but when one has noted a certain resemblance between the more complex forms of linenfold and the drapery-folds

*How unmistakeable can be judged by contrasting them with a small boarded chest in the little church of Saunderton, Bucks. This chest, which has an under-arching of quasi-Gothic design, is incised 'S G / 1754.'

on medieval figure-sculptures, one has said about all that is really pertinent to the matter.

As previously mentioned, the linenfold, though entirely medieval in conception, does not begin to appear until late in the fifteenth century. Its main popularity seems to have approximated to the reign of Henry VIII (1509-1547), but it continued to be used for many a long year, and in debased forms was known as late as the seventeenth century. In *Ancient Coffers and Cupboards* (1902; p.119) my father illustrated (from Arthur Radford's collection) an elaborate example of 1642. This retained all the average features, though in some other late instances the form is simplified almost beyond recognition. However rude they may be, such simplified pieces at least represent the continuity of an expiring tradition, and must not be confused with the recrudescence of this, among other medieval motifs, at the time of the Gothic Revival in the nineteenth century.

I have said that any sort of chest of an earlier date than Elizabeth's reign (1558-1603) is difficult to obtain; but this does not mean that true Elizabethan chests are in any way to be easily purchased. In fact, most of the so-called 'Elizabethan' furniture that comes on the market is actually later in period, belonging to various dates in the seventeenth century after her time. There was no sharp dividing line between the 'Elizabethan' and what is all too loosely called the 'Jacobean'. One can watch the style dying away, as it were, right down to the end of the century, by which time it had become altogether a country tradition. It is for this reason that chests bearing arcading or caryatids (terminal figures of semi-human form, Fig. 49),[9] the *guilloche*, strap-work and other ornament nominally Elizabethan in character, will often be found to date from some such period as the first or second quarters of the seventeenth century.

To discuss fine points of differentiation would be to lead the reader into severely technical byways; but one useful tip (to be used with due discrimination) concerns the size and shape of the panels. Under, say, Henry VIII, panels might be of various shapes, but not a few tended to length as opposed to breadth. Later in the sixteenth century, they tended to become small and square, this being noticeable of many Elizabethan chests. By Charles I's time, they had become taller and broader: a condition which more or less persisted while oak chests continued to be made in the traditional way. Attention should also be given to the important matter of mouldings as well as to other details which here must go by default. Chests and chests-of-drawers—we shall come to them later—with mitred mouldings arranged to form more or less elaborate patterns (Fig. 42) are usually attributable to the period of Charles II (1660-1685) though panels with shaped mouldings were known earlier and the type was continued to about the close of the seventeenth century. About that same end of the century, and persisting well into the eighteenth, we find another type of panel, with raised centre (itself usually an indication of lateness) and a shaped top, sometimes distantly reminiscent of a Gothic archhead. This, in so far as any Gothicness is concerned, was a revival rather than a tradition, though it also adds its scrap of evidence to support the contention that at no time has the Gothic entirely lapsed, however much it may have been misinterpreted by later generations. Such panels and their near relatives are most frequently found on settles and 'court cupboards' (real or so-called), though they also occur on chests, and may be compared with the shaped tops of long-case clock doors till almost the close of the eighteenth century. Yet another type of ornament of special interest is the tulip-motif, associated with the tulip-mania of the seventeenth century, when vast sums were paid for rare bulbs. (We may here remind ourselves of Dumas' romance *The Black Tulip*.) It is said that this craze was brought back by Charles II from his exile in Holland, though in fact the tulip-motif occurs, I believe, on furniture of a date somewhat earlier than 1660; as well it might in view of the detail that the mania was already rampant in Holland in 1639. On the other hand, furniture so carved may be later than the reign of the Merry Monarch. I recall seeing, many years ago, a part of a chest-front then exhibited in Aylesbury Museum, which was carved with conventional tulips and the legend 16EH92.[10] From my recollection of it, this mutilated waif almost certainly came from a country-made chest.

Knowledgeable readers will have noticed that, so far, I have made no attempt to differentiate between 'coffer' and 'chest'; and before we turn to other matters allusion should be made to this rather perplexing subject. Nowadays, coffer and chest are popularly regarded as interchangeable terms, the former having a pleasant air of antiquity. Actually, both words are ancient, though the precise distinction between them has yet to be fully explained. That such a definition existed is certain. To go back no earlier, at an unknown date between 1558 and 1579—a period fixed by Lord

Keeper Bacon's tenure of the Great Seal—my ancestor Anthony Rooe (or Roo) of Dallinghoo, Suffolk, was a party to a chancery suit claiming as heir certain lands in Melton in the same county. He alleged that those lands, which had been seized to his uncle Robert Rooe, had wrongly come into the hands of a certain yeoman, John Bray (or Braye) of Bradfield, and prayed for redress. Braye's answer was that the said Robert Rooe had indeed been so seized, but had released the property in 22nd Henry VIII to another John Braye from whom it had descended of right to the defendant. The parties then proceeded to call each other liars (in strictly legal phraseology)—after which, record of the suit irritatingly lapses.[11]

Now the weakness of Anthony's case (the rights of which I do not presume to assess) was evidently that he lacked documents. To cover this lack, his man-of-law resorted to a formula of which the counterpart is to be found in other ancient legal instruments. He said, in effect, that for as much as the certainty and number of the deeds, etc., were unknown to the Lord Keeper's orator (*i.e.* to Anthony), and whether in 'bagge or boxe sealed or in Cheste or Cofer locked', the said orator was without remedy by common law. With that recital, we may take our leave of Anthony and his grievance, remarking as we do so that allusion to 'Cheste or Cofer', not forgetting its balancing clause of 'bagge or boxe'. Obviously either chest or coffer was securable by one or more locks, and box or strong-room bag either actually or potentially so. Whether fancifully or not, we may perhaps detect some sort of a parallel between this marshalling of coffer and 'boxe', but to carry surmise further might be misleading. A barrister to whom I have referred this detail advises me of his certainty that neither 'chest' nor 'coffer' was 'a term of art in law and its meaning in any legal document would have depended on the circumstances in which it was used in each case. Either word would be held to mean whatever it originally meant in the language of the day unless there was something in the document in which it appeared to suggest that it was being used in a special way.'

Now it is fairly obvious that though our earlier ancestry was fully aware of a distinction between chest and coffer, that distinction became obscured. I do not suppose that many of our less remote ancestors were much better advised on the matter than are most of us to-day. My father believed that the distinction was mainly between the flush-fronted (boarded) or early framed receptacle, both of which he classed as 'coffers', and the panelled variety ('chests').

This somewhat broad definition has more in it than meets the eye. Elsewhere an attempt was made to show that coffers were *small* strong-boxes or caskets, but the case here was injured by old documentary allusions to *small coffers*, thus creating an obvious redundancy. (One may compare the analogous Italian term *antico cofanetto*.) More recently, Mr R. W. Symonds has adduced evidence to show that a coffer was a chest covered in leather or some other material and bound with iron.[12] This is, doubtless, correct as far as it goes, but that it holds good of all coffers (actual or so-called) at all periods seems to me dubious. That the coffer was properly a strong-chest is obvious, and many were certainly iron-bound, as witness an allusion to 'yren bounden coffres' in *Piers Plowman*. Such would tend, on the whole, to be of the 'flush' variety, and it appears to me to be possible that the word 'coffer' may have been loosely applied to chests built on the 'flush' principle, if not with the other concomitants of the true coffer. It would, perhaps, be permissible to call such pieces (*e.g.* boarded chests) 'coffer-type', and so do something to harmonize the various theories without violence to the facts.

Light of a sort is cast on this problem of coffer-construction by an heraldic reference which occurred to me when contemplating some data relating to my mother's family. In 1513 there died and was buried at Banbury a certain Sir William Cope, forebear of a well-known baronetical family and, incidentally, of the original builder of Holland House, Kensington—Cope's Castle, to give it its earlier name. This family of Cope was granted and still bears a pretty coat-of-arms in which *roses* and *fleurs-de-lys* symbolize the favour erstwhile enjoyed of the House of Tudor. But Sir William Cope was sometime Cofferer of the Household to Henry VII, and in that capacity he appears to have used a shield of *Argent*, 3 *Coffers sable*, *garnished or and vert*. A more or less contemporary rendering of this coat is preserved in the College of Arms (Alphabet L.2, p. 133, fig. 3) under the spelling of 'Coope'. This interesting record is reproduced in this book by permission of the Chapter of the College of Arms, and in view of Cope's official position it may be supposed that the coffers were rendered in an acceptable form (*page 40*).

Now, tinctures in heraldry are very often arbitrary (*e.g.* red or blue lions), so we may not hastily assume that the colours of the coffers are necessarily such as would have actually appeared. If Cope's coffers were really black (*sable*), the fact might give incidental support to Mr Symonds' contention that such pieces were leathered.* But as, in normal heraldic practice, it was unfeasible to show a black coffer with black (iron) straps, either gold or silver had to be employed, and it may be assumed that as gold is more regal than silver the former was used to indicate the metal fittings. Unless we appreciate this point, we might assume that a coffer was necessarily bound with brass or laton—a very unsafe deduction. Moreover, we need not suppose that *all* coffers were further garnished with ties of twisted strands (which could be sealed in place) as shown in the drawing. We may here remind ourselves that green and white were Tudor colours, in this case the green being suggested by the ties and the white by the silver field of the coat.

If this rendering of the Cofferer's arms of office does not answer our queries at all points, it at least shows that, in the sixteenth century, a flush-built and metal-guarded type of chest was accepted as a coffer. Even so, it still remains evident that, even then, all *coffers* were not of this kind. As much is shown by such a documentary reference as that reciting the New Year's day gift of 'Sir John A-lee' (Legh) to Queen Elizabeth, 1561-2. Legh's gift was 'a cofer of woode, carved, paynted, and gilt, with combes, glasses, and balls,' [13] seemingly some sort of dressing-case. It may, however, have been of 'flush' construction which, in my view, is one of the characteristics of a coffer, though the looseness with which the term was used is further suggested by the equation of 'chest or coffyn for the corse' in Sir Richard Clough's account in 1558-9 of the burial of the Emperor Charles V at Brussels. [14]

I may add that I am by no means convinced that many medieval chests, unbanded but of heavy construction, are to be excluded from the category known to our medieval forebears as coffers. One has merely to envisage a medieval treasury or muniment room, equipped in the manner of the Chapel of the Pyx at Westminster Abbey, to appreciate that an arbitrary distinction between types of strong-chest would have tended to lapse out of mind. If we have muddled 'coffer' and 'chest' we are no more to blame than a goodly pack of our ancestors.

A great many chests (and coffers) are equipped with a shallow

**cp.* 'my black cofer in the newe chambur.'—will of Richard Wrottesley, 1518. (Major-Gen. the Honble George Wrottesley: *History of the Family of Wrottesley of Wrottesley*, 1903, p. 255). Specification of the colour suggests that coffers were not always black.

tray fitted across the inside of one of the ends. This convenient adjunct has a long history; and it will occasionally be found that the tray is provided with a double bottom, forming a 'secret' for

The 'Coffers of Cope', showing how these receptacles were displayed in the arms, as Cofferer of the Household, of Sir William Cope (d. 1513). *From a MS. (Alphabet L.2, p. 133, fig. 3) in the College of Arms, by permission of the Chapter of the College.*

the concealment of small articles of value. The space between the floor of the tray and the true bottom is masked by the outer side of the tray, access being afforded by sliding the side upwards. In actual practice, these 'secrets' must have become fairly well known, and in many cases would not have defeated more than a cursory search. Even so, they doubtless served their purpose well enough as, though not common, they have survived in sufficient quantity to prove that they enjoyed a certain popularity.

As further illustrating the dual-purpose nature of much antique furniture, it should be added that the lid of this tray (when a lid is provided) is extremely useful, when raised, to support the open top of the chest itself. Anyone who has ever opened a heavy chest, especially when it is placed too close to a wall, will have quickly realized the double utility of the lidded tray within.

4 · Of Desks and Boxes

'IN bagge or boxe sealed' ran that clause in old Anthony's bill, and it reminds us of an earlier allusion, in the *Paston Letters*, wherein Thomas Playters, writing in April 1461, desires that John Paston's testament in a suit at law 'be sealed in a box and sent to me, and I shall keep it safe with God's grace.' Indeed, the habit of using small boxes for conveyance as well as for custody appears to have been as usual as the provision of 'trussing-coffers' for the transport of weightier loads. Examples of such boxes and skippets, some of them medieval, are preserved in the Public Record Office, London. Our present concern, however, is less with such as these as with that other near relation of the chest—the so-called 'Bible-Box'. This belonged to a class of furniture indiscriminately used in town and country, and whether a given example was made in one or the other is often not apparent. On the other hand, the obviously rustic character of a piece may enable one to dub it as country-made without fear of contradiction.

In the first place, it should be understood that 'Bible-Box' is collectors' jargon, based on the supposition that such receptacles were used to contain our forebears' scanty libraries. It is by no means impossible, and even probable, that some of them fulfilled such a purpose. Few folk of the lesser sort, to say nothing of many better placed in the world, had much in the way of books. A box of small dimensions would have been quite enough to hold the very few volumes that were all the private library of that master of English prose, John Bunyan. At the same time, we must not too readily take for granted the booklessness of smaller homes. Always were there modest scholars whose patient labour has in some instances enriched the knowledge of later generations. Such a man was possibly a certain Dennis Grundie, of Rumworth, in the parish of Deane, near Bolton, Lancs., who in 1633 bequeathed to one of his sons, Joseph, 'all his Greek and Latin books'.[15] Such, certainly, was the Rev. Thomas Delafield (1690-1759), curate of Fingest and schoolmaster of Stokenchurch, in Bucks, whose manuscripts are now preserved in the Bodleian, and who 'preserved a family legend . . . that his ancestor was Mr Delafield the surgeon who tended the last moments of John Hampden as he lay dying in the inn at Thame'.[16] A scant box or so would never have housed the collections of such village scholars as these.

Admitting that, in the words of J. R. Green's *History of the English People*, 'No greater moral change ever passed over a nation than passed over England during the years which parted the middle of the reign of Elizabeth from the meeting of the Long Parliament,' when 'England became the people of a book, and that book was the Bible', we are still without warranty that the great majority of the things we now call 'Bible-Boxes' were made to any such end. They might have served any useful purpose, and some, especially those of unusually long formation, were more probably meant to hold lace or small articles of attire. Of such were the 'lace-chests' as used by lacemakers in Buckinghamshire and elsewhere. However, when we speak of a 'Bible-Box' we have a mental picture of the sort of thing as shown in Fig. 6 and in so far the popular label is not without its convenience. I do not include here any description of certain true Bible-Boxes, made in the outward semblance of a book to encase the sacred volume, and such as is represented by a Dutch-Singhalese box of calamander wood in the Victoria and Albert Museum. A somewhat similar idea is seen in an early sixteenth-century carved pearwood case for a book in the Wallace Collection; but this is German, and I am not aware that the like device gained any hold in England, though Dr Charles R. Beard has an English brass tobacco-box of *circa* 1645, made in the form of a small volume.[17] There are, of course, the Book-Boxes made out of actual volumes, or in a similar manner with binder's work: one method being to form a cavity in a book by cutting away the centre of the pages, and then lining it, leaving the covers and glued-together edges intact. This, when placed on a shelf, is indistinguishable from other books and affords a ready means of keeping or concealing papers or small objects; but, though such boxes were made in the past, a good many of those on the market are of recent manufacture, though the volumes concerned may be old. Our present concern is wholly with the rectangular boxes to which the name of 'Bible-Box' has been somewhat too readily applied.

Of the 'Bible-Boxes' within an average collector's reach almost none is older, and some are later, than the seventeenth century. I myself have a box (from Essex) of which the front, carved with dolphin-like scrolls, enclosed in a roped border, may be as old as the time of Henry VIII, though the rest of the (anciently assembled) box is less certainly of sixteenth-century date (Fig. 6). *Per contra*, in the Museum at High Wycombe there is an undecorated example lettered C W 1798. But the most typical 'Bible-Boxes' are of seventeenth-century fashion. Their carved or incised ornament is consistent with the styles obtaining in that period, and they proffer a fair field for study as none but quite outstanding examples are reckoned much of by professional buyers. I have various interesting examples, one of which has all the appearance of being not only a country piece, but a home-made piece at that (Fig. 6). Formerly in the Townroe Collection, it is boldly and roughly carved with the lunette ornament so frequently found on seventeenth-century furniture, the space between the opposing curves of the lunettes being occupied by a small mask, moustachioed and royalled (or bearded), of a type recalling the so-called 'mortuary masks' of Charles I on certain chairs of equivalent date. I shall have more to say about these chairs in their due place; but this box clinches the date by displaying it in bold characters ANNODO[ ]MMI1652, the DOMMI being the carver's way of spelling *Domini*. Thus we know that this box was made in the year of Our Lord 1652, three years after the execution of Charles I. It will be noticed that the incised spandrels are filled with Gothic leaf-ornament of a kind that had lingered on from the fifteenth century, perhaps receiving reinforcement from that Revival known to us as 'Carolean Gothic'. But though distinctly Gothic in type, such leaf-spandrels have also a classic ancestry. They occur, for example, on the well-known gravestone, now in Colchester Castle, of Marcus Favonius Facilis, a member of the Pollia *gens*, and a centurion of the XXth Legion. This memorial of the first century A.D. was found at Colchester in 1868; but in mentioning it we must not argue any connection between it and the box of 1652. Idle hands at a later date have scored initials on the box I H E (in column), and H (or B) T; but all concerned have long since been gathered to the narrow cells in which 'the rude Forefathers of the hamlet sleep'.

Some collectors make little attempt to differentiate between the 'Bible-Box' and the Desk, which, of course, could quite well have been used for similar purposes. As Mr Charles H. Hayward has reminded us in his *English Period Furniture* (ed. 1947; p. 63), the slope in sundry cases may have been used for convenience in reading rather than writing, and certain examples (*e.g.* Fig. 45) lend colour to this theory, though it is not one which should be pushed too far in the face of the iconographical evidence. On the whole, the desk with its sloping top forms a distinct type which is better kept separate, though its relationship to the box on the one hand is as clear as is its relationship to the bureau on the other.

So far as oak is concerned, the desks available to the average buyer very seldom ante-date the seventeenth century, many of them belonging to the second half of that period. Almost all of them are independent, that is they are Table Desks, made without stands. Indeed, it will be generally found that when oak desks of this character are provided with stands, either the substructure is of a later period, or else the desk and its base have been 'married'. To find Desks-on-Stands—made as such—one has usually to seek for examples in other woods and from no earlier a date than the latter part of the seventeenth century onwards. On the other hand, such a piece as the famous standing desk from Stratford-upon-Avon Grammar School, now in Shakespeare's Birthplace, would alone conclusively prove that Table Desks were not the sole variety made. The oak Table Desk has a long history, and its more modern use was perpetuated in the mahogany folding contraptions, often inset with a plaque of mother-of-pearl or some other substance in the centre of the lid. In my parents' salad-days, it was every young person's ambition to have his or her own desk, equipped with inkwell and pen-tray, and a space below the slope to hold papers. I still have my mother's and my father's desks—typically Victorian pieces of occasional furniture—which eventually became mere places of storage for 'dead' correspondence of personal interest. Such desks as these do not yet appeal to collectors, but at least they perpetuate an ancient tradition.

Of the desks of an earlier generation, it is also noticeable that very few of them have a ledge to prevent the paper laid on them from slipping. It is clear from old prints and pictures, that, when in use, the paper was held in place by the hand unoccupied with the pen—a proceeding that may well strike us as inconvenient, but which did not trouble the original users. One desk in my possession, boldly carved with debased ornament of Jacobean type is dated 1682, the corresponding position on the other side of the lock-plate being blank, though obviously reserved for carving. This suggests that one could go to a shop and select one's piece, having one's initials added as required. In this case, for some unknown reason, the marks of identity were never added (Fig. 7).

Another desk, of similar character, now in my wife's possession, is fully carved with initials I W 1692; and thereby hangs a tale. For this desk was found at one end of Gloucester Road in South Kensington; and, at the other end, on another occasion, there turned up a late chest with the same initials and the date [16]95 (Fig. 5).[18] A nearer approach to a match scarcely occurs once in a blue moon, though whether or not there was any original association between the two pieces is a matter for conjecture. If I have no absolute warranty for describing these as 'country', they were at least made when oak had been displaced by walnut, and are in no sense modish pieces.

Among other types of box-furniture suited to the cottage or farmhouse, may be rapidly noted such matters as the Knife-Box, the Candle-Box, the Salt-Box, and the little Bobbin-Box in which the lacemaker's bobbins were kept when not in use. There is also the standing rectangular flour-bin or kneading-trough, now sometimes dignified to superior purposes in the home. Certain of the more elaborately fashioned of these troughs are not without their decorative appeal, though some of those I have seen on the market were certainly not English. Of such smaller fry as the knife-, candle-, and salt-boxes not much need be said. Many of the more obviously rural examples are made in oak, and some possess the argeeable simplicity of leather hinges. Such boxes are mostly of late period, say eighteenth century, or even later. One cylindrical type of candle-box, frequently found in metal examples of no particular age, is also known to me from an example in oak, found in Essex. In this case, however, the body was not a true cylinder, but polygonal, built up of short strips of wood with a shaped back serving as a hanger.

The Salt-Box, once indispensable in every kitchen, is usually a plain affair; but, modest as it is, this essentially utilitarian article is not without its literature. It was once made the subject of a mock-examination paper attributed to no less than the erudite Richard Porson (1759-1808), Regius Professor of Greek at Cambridge University, and intended as a satire on the contemporary method of examination at Oxford. The curious will find it in full in a little book by 'Socius' entitled *Facetiae Cantabrigienses*, of which the third edition (1836) is before me. With incredible gravity, it treats of its subject—the common or household salt-box—under three headings: *Metaphysics*, *Logic*, and *Natural Philosophy*.

The paper is too long to be quoted in full, but two extracts may whet the appetite of those who relish inspired nonsense. For example, under *Metaphysics* :—

Professor. What is a salt-box?

Student. It is a box made to contain salt.

Professor. How is it divided?

Student. It is a salt-box and a box of salt.

Professor. Very well; show the distinction?

Student. A salt-box may be where there is no salt; but salt is absolutely necessary to the existence of a box of salt.

Professor. Are not salt-boxes otherwise divided?

Student. Yes, by a partition.

Professor. What is the use of this division?

Student. To separate the *coarse* from the *fine*.

Professor. How! Think a little.

Student. To separate the *fine* from the *coarse*.

Professor. To be sure. . . . But are not salt-boxes otherwise distinguished?

Student. Yes, into possible, probable, and positive. . . . A possible salt-box is a salt-box yet unsold in the joiner's hands . . . [a probable salt-box is] in the hands of one going to buy salt, and who has sixpence in his pocket to pay the shopkeeper; and a positive salt-box is one which hath actually and *bonâ fide* got salt in it.

Professor. Very good; and what other divisions of the salt-box do you recollect?

Student. They are divided into *substantive* and *pendent*. A substantive salt-box is that which stands by itself on a table or dresser; and the pendent is that which hangs against the wall. . . .

And again, under *Natural Philosophy* :—

Professor. What is a salt-box?

Student. It is a combination of matter, fitted, framed, and joined, by the hands of a workman, in the form of a box, and adapted for the purpose of receiving and containing salt.

Professor. Very good. What are the *mechanical powers* engaged in the construction of a salt-box?

Student. The *axe*, the *saw*, the *plane*, and the *hammer* . . .

Professor. Is the *saw* only used in slitting timber into boards?

Student. Yes; it is also used in cutting boards into lengths.

Professor. Not lengths. A thing cannot be said to be cut into lengths.

Student. Shortnesses.

Professor. Very right . . .

Reading this stuff—and I have wilfully omitted some of the drollest passages—who can wonder that it took an Oxford don and a profound mathematician to give us *Alice's Adventures in Wonderland*! All the same, having digested those extracts, it would be a dull fellow who can find no interest whatever in a salt-box.

Yet another type of partitioned box is the club or tavern Tobacco-box, the lock of which is operated by pressing a coin through a slot, thus enabling a smoker to fill his pipe by paying for it.

> The custom is, before you fill,
> To put a penny in the till ;
> When you have filled, without delay,
> Close the lid or sixpence pay.

Such boxes are usually found in metal, but wooden examples are not unknown. One specimen with shaped tops to its sides suggests a date about the junction of the seventeenth and eighteenth centuries, or, more probably, in the early part of the eighteenth. It is neatly made and finished, even the locking device, except for one or two details, being wooden. Such pieces are, however, distinctly unusual, though examples in brass are somewhat less so, the latter usually being considerably later in date than the rare and relatively early item noted above (Fig. 8).

As illustrating how boxes (of any sort) may be found in unexpected places, a minor discovery announced in the *Evening Standard*, 7th November 1933, is not without interest. By the account, a Mr Norton, son of a miller at Meopham in Kent, happened to find a small wooden box 'under a beam in the old windmill' overlooking the village green. The box was 'filled with cricketing records, pencilled in little books and on scraps of paper,' the records being 'those of the late Mr T. Killick, a miller, and once secretary of the village cricket club'.

They showed that 'in 1822 the club played seven matches. On practice nights the players were fined one penny if they missed a catch, while committee members were liable to a fine of sixpence if they did not attend a meeting'. Unfortunately, the account of this salutary discipline is unaccompanied by any further description of the box itself, or by any explanation as to why it should have been concealed with a care more proper to the lodgement of 'dangerous documents'.

5 · Of Chairs and Chair-Tables

AS nearly as I can now say, it was in 1903 or '04, that my father made a stupendous discovery. He had been out on one of his trips—sketching and 'kernoozing'[19]—to the country, and returned in a state of high excitement. He had discovered that rarity of rarities—a Gothic chair. I naturally asked where the treasure had been found, and was perfectly satisfied when he told me that the place was called 'Diddlesham'. Like many of the older breed of collectors, my father at that time preferred to keep his hunting-grounds to himself.

However, in later years, he gave me the story in detail. It was something like this :—

He, as I after him, had an affection for the ancient market-town of Aylesbury, and it was while strolling in one of its streets that he passed a house-door, standing open what time a serving-maid was engaged on some duties. Standing in the passage was a good chest of the time of Henry VIII, its panels carved with those projecting heads of the type known anciently as 'Romayne work'.

Pausing, my father sent in his card to the householder, and asked for an interview. There was other old oak in evidence, and tactful questioning elicited the fact that its owner might not be averse to parting with a piece or so. The owner (I withhold his name) was by way of being some sort of a bailiff or overseer to a renowned family, and in the course of his journeyings in the county he had chances to purchase pieces of oak, which he liked and which, in those days, were not nearly as much esteemed as they are now.

To a question as to whether he had any chests with linenfold panels, the owner thought for a moment, and then said no; but come and have a look in the loft. He conducted my father to a loft approached by a ladder.[20] And there, grey with age and exposure, stood a veritable Gothic chair—or at any rate one dating from the time of the first Tudor to mount the throne of England. It was the chair illustrated on p. 61 of my father's *Old Oak Furniture* (1905), and it cost him all of £2 10s. od. !

There may be among my readers some who are unversed in the hazards of collecting. I wonder how I can bring home to such readers the true inwardness of this discovery? Simply one cannot buy genuine Gothic chairs for love or money. For the most part, they just don't exist. One might almost as well go searching for the world's largest diamond or the original Crown of St. Edward the Confessor in the nearest pawnshop. You *may* have luck, but the odds against you are astronomical. I do not myself doubt that this chair had been all along in the county where it was so happily found. But a more cogent reason for mentioning it here is that in construction it is aligned with the slab-ended method already encountered on chests of the boarded variety. Each of the sides is formed of a single massive slab of oak, the tops shaped as arm-rests, and pierced with lifting-grips. The chair-back and the front of the box-seat are framed, with well executed linenfold panels. The locker beneath the seat had lost its door which was at the rear; and the seat itself had at some time been mutilated by the cutting of a hole necessary for its conversion to close-chair. These minor imperfections were made good; otherwise, the piece was in perfect condition.

Again let me warn the reader that any similar discovery is highly improbable. For practical purposes, the collector of country furniture can take it that it will only be by outstanding good fortune that he can acquire any antique chair pre-dating the seventeenth century. And if he *does* light upon an Elizabethan example, or one of Elizabethan character, it may be difficult to decide whether or not it is in the fullest sense a country piece. For example, the armchair in Fig. 9 is stated to have come from a family of farmers at Pateley Bridge, Nidderdale, Yorks, and the tradition of it is that the initials W B carved on its back stand for 'William Bland'.[21] There certainly were, and doubtless are, Blands in Yorkshire, and it is just possible that the chair was made for a member of a collateral branch of the same stock that produced the well-known baronetical house of Bland of Kippax Park. In style, the chair, if not marked by any great refinement, is scarcely bucolic; but, remembering William Harrison's account of farmers' prosperity under Elizabeth, we must not too hastily assume that such a piece would have been above the reach of a superior yeoman, though it would have been equally suited to persons of loftier quality. One rare and interesting feature of this chair, with its richly arcaded back, is that to the left of the base of the W initial is neatly incised a small capital G, presumably a maker's mark as it has none of the air of the random scratchings sometimes inflicted on furniture after it was made.

As said, most of the earlier chairs that still await the collector are of seventeenth-century date, the more countrified examples following the prevalent styles, though sometimes at a distance. Their main stylistic tendencies can be recognized from almost any of the general histories of English furniture, so we need not cross well-trodden ground in closely tracing them. We watch the 'Elizabethan' persisting well after the death of the Virgin Queen, and shading off into the 'Jacobean' and 'Carolean', but when we meet the 'Commonwealth' we encounter one variety deserving of special mention—the so-called 'Mortuary Chairs' of Derbyshire and Yorkshire.[22] It is by no means certain that their descriptive title is more than a piece of modern jargon, but the tradition behind them may have somewhat to commend it. These chairs, many of them dating from the 1650's or a trifle later, have distinctive backs with a couple of arched backrests of escalloped outline (Fig. 10). In the centre of each of these rests will sometimes be found carved a small moustachioed and royalled mask, said to represent King Charles I, who lost his head in 1649. There may be something in the notion. At any rate, it is far more probable than a counter-suggestion that these heads were off-shoots of the bearded masks so frequently found on 'Greybeard' or 'Bellarmine' jugs (Fig. 52); and that the chairs embody an allusion to the celebrated Cardinal Bellarmine (who died in 1621) can be disregarded. It should be added that the term 'Mortuary Chair' has no relation to a dead-house. It embodies an old use of 'mortuary' indicating, in the words of the *Oxford English Dictionary*, 'Of, concerned with or depending upon death; relating to or reminiscent of death.' The trophies of arms and banners erected over tombs in bygone times were 'mortuaries'; and certain swords of the Civil War period bearing heads of, or supposedly of, Charles I and his Consort, are known to collectors as 'Mortuary Swords', though this, as in the case of the chairs, may be a coined term. It should here be mentioned that 'Mortuary Chairs' are among the types that have been freely reproduced in modern times.

Oak furniture continued to be made in the country long after it had been ousted from the fashionable world by walnut and, later, by mahogany. That does not mean that all oak furniture of the late seventeenth and the eighteenth centuries was actually made in rural areas. A good deal of it, growing progressively scantier as time advanced, would have been made for the less exclusive town uses;

though town and country were still near together, and an interchange of goods either way must be allowed for. For average country usage, much resort was had not only to oak, but to elm, beech, ash, cherry and sundry other woods, each with its own beauty but not in demand for the more modish products. Thus it was that, at a time when such houses as Vile and Cobb, Manwaring, Chippendale and various other of the more exclusive town firms were producing splat-chairs of mahogany, lesser makers (including their country cousins) were busily turning out more or less equivalent pieces of the types seen in Figs. 13 and 14. It would be idle to pretend that such chairs approach the real 'town' pieces in quality; but they are often well designed, honest, and by far the more suitable to a cottage or small country-dwelling. For one thing, their surfaces are nothing like so easily impaired.

The presence of a deep wooden apron below the seat of a chair is usually a sign that the piece is, or was, a Close- or Commode-Chair, the purpose of the apron being to screen the pan of metal (such as pewter) or glazed pottery. Close-Chairs and Close-Stools (of which anon in Chapter VI) are still in use, especially by invalids, but before the general introduction of sanitation they must have been even more favoured. Indeed, enough antique examples have survived to suggest that they were made in fairly considerable quantities. Occasionally an out-of-date piece, such as the rare late Gothic chair discussed at the beginning of the present chapter, was converted, by mutilation of the seat, to Close-Chair; but obtainable Close-Chairs, made as such, are mostly no earlier than the eighteenth century. Some persons see fit to remove or curtail the apron, but such action should be discouraged as, other objections apart, it falsifies the proportions of the chair. Close-Chairs were made in varying sizes and degrees of quality—examples intended for children are found—and of the various types some are evidently of country origin.

Country chairs in general now find so ready a market, that one looks back wistfully to the days when nobody wanted them. When I was still a boy, a large store in Kensington had somehow acquired literally masses of old country chairs, many of eighteenth-century date. I remember seeing them stacked on top of each other from floor to ceiling—pick as you please at 5/- a chair! Almost any one of them would now command an average figure of £4 or £5. I managed to buy a couple out of my limited pocket-money, and only wish I had had the means and inclination to 'stock-up' with more. My father helped me to choose a couple of decent examples. Fig. 14 shows them.

Chairs of this kind are frequently labelled as 'Country Chippendale', a misleading term merely convenient as indicating the general style of the piece. If the firm of Chippendale could not possibly have produced the vast array of furniture since dubbed with its title, it is equally certain that the mass of 'Country Chippendale' must be split up among the numerous local craftsmen, most of whom are now completely forgotten by name. The same applies to country manifestations of Hepplewhite, Sheraton, Adam or Regency. Assuredly it, too, applies to that type of chair so prevalent in country districts and not exempt from town usage, the 'Windsor'.

This is primarily a stick-back, wooden-seated chair, with turned or plain legs, and often (though not necessarily) having a decorative splat in the back. The seat is very frequently shaped, and more or less saddle-formed, though a circular seat is occasionally found. At a late period, the stick-back was challenged by designs of a different order, as can be seen by a comparison of Figs. 16-17.

There is an old and crusted story to the effect that, one rainy afternoon, King George III sheltered in a cottage near Windsor Castle, and took a liking to the type of chair he found there. Such is held by some to account for the name of 'Windsor Chair'; but (as Mr Symonds has shown[23]) the name is certainly much older than that, and it is plain enough that the type itself was already well established. Indeed it is held by some that this type of stick-back chair is a modified off-shoot of a medieval form of high antiquity, which may be one reason why Windsors have a happy knack of harmonizing with so many other pieces of widely different styles and periods.

Leaving aside its early origins, we can claim for the Windsor a continuity of tradition from the latter part of the seventeenth century till to-day. In this sense, the earliest form is that with a cresting fitted to the top of the back-sticks (*e.g.* Fig. 16). Among varieties of this form is the 'Goldsmith Chair', so-called for no better reason than because a well-known mid-eighteenth-century example of it (in the Victoria and Albert Museum) is stated to have belonged to Oliver Goldsmith. Crested Windsors continued to be made in the second half of the century, but by this time the more familiar bent-wood hooped back was in being (Fig. 16 and page 55). Eighteenth-century Windsors of both types sometimes have cabriole legs instead of the stick or turned variety. A sought-after form of chair is that with a back of an acutely arched outline, and with details inspired by what then passed muster as 'Gothick'. In all types, the splats proffer a rather wide field of choice, one of the most interesting being that with the *plumes d'ostruce*—'badge for Peace' of the Heir Apparent (Fig. 16). It is believed that this device was borrowed from one much affected by the firm of Hepplewhite, and it should be stressed that its use on furniture was (in the main) patriotic and not at all necessarily an indication of princely ownership. The Prince of Wales alluded to was, of course, the 'First Gentleman in Europe'—the gorgeous being who later became King George IV. But perhaps the most common type of Windsor splat is that with a wheel- or boss-centre, examples of which may belong to any date from the end of the eighteenth century to our own times (page 55). I have noted as a matter of practical experiment, that some modern Windsors, though closely following traditional patterns, are somewhat skimped and a shade ungenerous in their proportions.

It must not be supposed that such chairs exhaust the list of Windsors, which leads away into types of a less readily recognizable character. An examination of the old pattern-books and illustrated price-lists of High Wycombe makers—(*e.g. Antique and Plain and Ornamental Modern Chairs.* Alfred Reeves and Co., Printers, 18, Finsbury Street, Chiswell Street, London, E.C. [*n.d.*])—proves that quite a number of nineteenth-century types were grouped under the 'Windsor' headings: stick-back, lath-back, baluster-and-spindle, Roman-spindle among them. A glance at Sir Lawrence Weaver's *High Wycombe Furniture* (1929), and at page 55 in the present book, is instructive on this point, though it is difficult to agree with Weaver that some of these late forms were 'primitive' —except in a purely colloquial sense.

All these represent a reversion from the hooped-back to the earlier crested form, though in detail they differ considerably from the earlier crested varieties. This applies to the backs, as, in general, the legs and seats follow the traditional Windsor pattern. There are, however, Victorian Windsors in which a more bulky type of faceted baluster-leg was introduced. I have seen and used large, heavy, undeniably comfortable lath-back Windsors of this type, which are furnished with splats in the tradition of the second half of the eighteenth century. Though the rest of the chairs had changed almost beyond recognition, the splats had continued to be made in the old way as a matter of course—another instance of traditional usage.

Windsor scroll-backs—in which the back uprights are scrolled over at the top, as in Fig. 17 (right)—are a humble version of a

Some *Windsor* chair-splats. *Left to right:* Pierced Baluster, about mid-eighteenth century; second half of eighteenth century; wheel-splat, late eighteenth-early nineteenth century. The dates are provisional, as some splats continued in use for a long while. The wheel-splat has been continued to modern times.

Top right: Windsor Armchair of Gothic type, second half of eighteenth century. Such chairs have been cleverly copied.

Right: Interlaced Bow Windsor, a simpler Gothic type, late eighteenth-early nineteenth century. Modern examples are known.

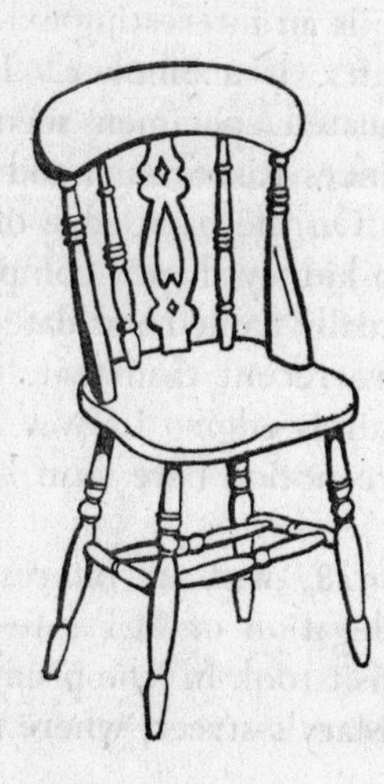

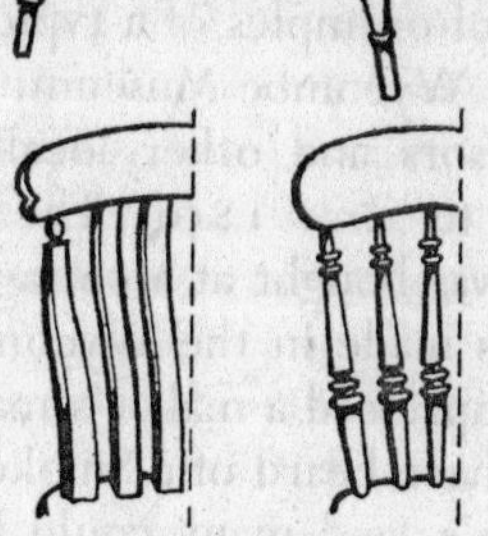

Late Windsor types, nineteenth century, some continuing into the twentieth. *Left to right*: Baluster and Spindle (the splat retaining eighteenth-century characteristics); Stick-Back; Lath Back; Roman Spindle.

Drawings by Frances Roe from various sources, and partly based on Weaver: *High Wycombe Furniture* (London: The Fanfare press, 1929).

Regency type, and as such their design is referable to the early part of the nineteenth century. Since, however, these chairs continued to be made for a long while, it is advisable not to be too optimistic in dating any that do not carry clear evidence of being other than traditional. The earliest only have any claim to be classed as antique, though as they are growing older every day even somewhat dubiously old examples may be tolerantly accepted as good, useful pieces with some sort of a background. Few of them are of much financial account as yet. Indeed, a rough example was recently reported to me as having been offered for sale in a county town for no more than five shillings; not that this price can be taken as a standard. One might easily have to pay more.

Among other Windsor types, one frequently found is the all-wood Corner-Chair (otherwise known as 'Smoker's Bow') with its Windsor legs and low back of semi-circular plan, supported by turned bobbins (Fig. 17). This is a homely descendant of the eighteenth-century Corner-Chair, itself made in various grades from the aristocratic to the humble, and it is mainly in the Windsor form that it has become a traditional item of furniture in the cottage, the pub., the office, the schoolroom. So far as I have observed them, most old examples date from no earlier than the first half of the nineteenth century, but, as the type has persisted to quite modern times, it is not always easy to be sure of the exact period of a given example. Many are more or less recent. I could name a comfortable bar in a Devonshire inn where there are a number of examples of a typically nineteenth-century goutiness. In the High Wycombe Museum, where there is an interesting exhibit of Windsors and other locally made chairs, is a Smoker's Bow assigned to *circa* 1850. The more attenuated specimen seen in Fig. 17 was bought at a cottage-sale in Princes Risborough and was doubtless made in the Wycombe district. On the back edge of its seat is impressed a maker's mark: DH in a kidney-shaped compartment. I have heard of a Smoker's Bow actually named and dated in the 1880's, and many could be even more recent than that. It is because this undeniably handy type of chair is edging its way into the antique category that it receives more notice here than is its proportionate due.

In the *Bucks Free Press* for 9th July 1948, was an interesting account of a visit by a Parliamentary delegation of M.P.s to the High Wycombe furniture industry. This visit took in 'the premises of Messrs Nicholls and Janes, Ltd., in St. Mary's-street, where they saw some of the few remaining hand carvers in the Wycombe industry still working in the first chair-making factory ever opened in the town—a tiny two-storey building* in St. Mary's-street, established in 1810 by Mr Thomas Widgington, great-great-grandfather of Mr R. W. Boreham, who is now director and secretary of Nicholls and Janes, Ltd.'

This is valuable information, though I take it to refer to the initiation of a factory-system for the manufacture of whole chairs, rather than to the start of chairmaking or the manufacture of chair-parts in or around Wycombe. In his *High Wycombe Furniture*, Sir Lawrence Weaver told us that 'Samuel Treacher and Thomas Widgington seem to have been the Chippendales of the Windsor Chair in the last quarter of the eighteenth century'; and J. J. Sheahan probably touched the heart of the matter in his *History and Topography of Buckinghamshire* (1862), when he quoted an article on chair-making from *Knight's British Almanack* :—

In a happy hour the people dwelling amidst the beech woods of the Chilterns took to chairmaking, and so vigorously pursued the occupation that the Buckinghamshire weed is becoming scarce. . . . It is remarkable how suddenly manufactures are localised under favourable circumstances. Chairs were, no doubt, always made in these districts. The Windsor chair has a fame of some antiquity; but the Wycombe chairmaking trade was scarcely known as something remarkable twenty or thirty years ago [*i.e.—circa* 1832-42, but these are very approximate figures]. The demand for the chairs has grown with the enormous increase of general population; the facilities of communication with the metropolis; the rapidly extending demand of our colonies. 'When I began the trade,' said a large manufacturer to me, 'I loaded a cart and travelled to Luton. All there was prosperous. There was a scramble for my chairs; . . .' This manufacturer now sends his chairs to London, Liverpool, and Manchester; to Australia, New Zealand, and Constantinople. He made 8,000 chairs for the Crystal Palace . . .

Other evidence of the nineteenth-century boom in Wycombe chairs is afforded by the formation in 1855 of the High Wycombe Chairmakers' Protection Society, with an ornamental membership card designed by Owen Mead. A specimen of this card, made out for one John Scott in December, 1855, is in High Wycombe Museum. It is a pretentious piece of trade heraldry, with shield and supporters, and 'in pretence', as the heralds say, a Victorian chair, though this is not a Windsor, but belongs to the type known in the industry as a 'balloon-back', of no present collector's interest. The President of the Society was then Robert White, with William Busby as Vice-President, and Mead himself as Secretary. On all

*[This is now a part of the larger premises of Messrs Nicholls & Janes].

accounts therefore, the great rise of the Wycombe chair industry is assignable to the nineteenth-century boom, but that it was practised much earlier, if not specially in Wycombe, at any rate 'in the hills', is attested by the occurrence of many chairs of pre-nineteenth century date.

What may well be a surviving trace of this older craft is found in the bodgers who for time out of mind have worked in the Chiltern beech-woods, turning chair-legs which they 'fed' to the chair-makers. Their method was the primitive one of erecting a shack which they moved from place to place as they cleared the ground of usable timber. Turning was done with a simple pole-lathe, an example of which is now in High Wycombe Museum.

A few practitioners of the bodger's venerable craft are still to be found at work. In the above-quoted issue of the *Bucks Free Press*, it is further recorded how the Parliamentary delegation was 'taken into the heart of the Hampden Woods . . . up a rough cart track to a primitive hut, where two of the last remaining Buckinghamshire chair bodgers, Mr Owen Dean and his brother Alec, were turning chair legs from beech trees by means of the pole lathe.' I have heard, however, of a bodger who has not stuck at introducing a power-driven lathe, so that modern methods are finding their way into a craft almost as remote as the Brandon flint-knapper's. This is, no doubt, as efficient as it is unavoidable, though one hopes that all trace of the time-honoured way will not eventually vanish. Again to quote Weaver, 'the machine cannot beat handicraft at making and turning a leg.' It is the machine that gives to furniture an air of mechanical regularity.

To appreciate this, one has merely to contrast the average commercial chair, however produced under current conditions, with the handiwork of such a master of the craft as Mr Harold Edward (known to his intimates as 'Jack') Goodchild, of Naphill, a straggling village in the wooded countryside between High Wycombe and Princes Risborough. Mr Goodchild, who with his picturesque workshop has been the subject of an admirable etching by Mr Stanley Anderson, R.A., and who has been made otherwise known by various literary, film and broadcast references, comes of a family long associated with the chair-making industry. He is himself capable of making any variety of Windsor, and is still (1949) prosecuting his work as vigorously as present conditions permit. This modest master-craftsman, who loves his vocation for what he can 'learn' from it, has made Windsors of all the well-known traditional types, and made them with an excellence and a niceness of judgment not merely equal to the finest antique examples, but much superior to many, whether old or new. It is very desirable that this should be widely bruited as, in the future, 'Goodchild Windsors' will undoubtedly be ranked with the finest of any period, not merely reproducing faithfully all the old characteristics, but doing so with a rare elegance and finish. I account it a privilege to have taken the capable hand that has brought into being so many rural masterpieces.

But though High Wycombe and its surrounding country can fairly claim a pre-eminence in the world of Windsors, it was very far from being the only area where such chairs were made. They were produced in parts as widely separated as Somerset, Yorkshire, Mendlesham in Suffolk and Scole in Norfolk; and a homely example in Fig. 16 I believe came from Wales. Mr Goodchild has mentioned to me the possibility of some having been made in the Cotswolds. Indeed they might be found almost anywhere; and an American authority[24] has recognized that the large and much appreciated body of Windsors in that country originated from England. 'American craftsmen seized on the idea,' adapting it to their own purposes, and very well they did so. (It would not altogether surprise me if the supply of true Colonial Windsors were augmented by discreet importations in more recent times, but let that pass!) As to 'Mendlesham Chairs', Mr R. W. Symonds elicited the pleasing detail that these are still known as 'Dan Day Chairs', after a local chairmaker named Daniel Day, whose son 'about 1790 is said to have worked for Thomas Sheraton, afterwards returning to his father's workshop'.[25]

As to materials, Windsors are often composed of more than one wood: oak, walnut, beech, ash, elm, yew, and fruitwoods are the ingredients from which the makers drew their timber for one of the most agreeable kinds of homely chair that England has to show.

Other sightly types of chair are to be found among the mass of ladder-back and spindle-back varieties, frequently equipped with rush-seats contrasting with the wooden, often saddle-shaped, seats characteristic of Windsors. Plain ladder-backs must have been made in large quantities in the eighteenth century and later (Fig. 18); but, even if one were to indulge in a parade of technicalities, or point out that a chair recognizably similar, though of course different in detail, was known in medieval times, there is not much that need be said about them here. Somewhat less common are the 'spindle-' or 'bobbin-backs,' with their inset rows of small, turned members. There are two main types of this sort of chair; that with a shaped cresting rail and that without. The first piece of furniture I ever bought was a nice example of the former variety, with bun-feet and a well-turned front-stretcher (Fig. 15). It cost somewhere about a sovereign, of which I managed to save fifteen shillings out of my pocket money. This is an eighteenth-century piece, though some chairs of pretty much the same sort can be assigned to the early part of the next century. Such chairs are frequently called 'Lancashire', where doubtless they were favoured, though the type is widely distributed. The kind more specifically associated with the County-Palatine is that on which the spindles are grouped rather to the centre of the row, leaving noticeable spaces open at each end. Sometimes, however, there are three rows of spindles, the centre row being entirely filled, and the others on the principle indicated above. It should be added that many spindle-backs have a simpler top than the decidedly eighteenth-century form of cresting shown in Fig. 15.

In some degree, the spindle-backs suggest a relationship with an earlier type in which turnery had become rampant. These 'thrown' chairs, usually triangular, are freely attributed to the Tudor period, but, though they doubtless represent a much more ancient form, many of the obtainable examples may be no earlier than the seventeenth century, though a few are possibly sixteenth, and lingering survivals of the type are found in the eighteenth. An elaborate example of turned ash and oak is in the Victoria and Albert Museum (W. 24—1913), where it has been loosely assigned to the sixteenth or seventeenth century, though I incline to the view that the earlier part of the seventeenth century is the more probable. The main locale of such pieces seems to have been 'in the West Country, the Marches of Wales, in Herefordshire, Lancashire and Cheshire'.[26] The character of some of them inclined my father to suspect a Scandinavian influence filtering down the Severn Valley. One well-known example of this type of chair was in Cheshunt Great House, where it was known as 'Cardinal Wolsey's Chair', and it was probably this attribution that encouraged the ascription of various other examples to the period of Henry VIII. Still better-known is the interesting chair in Leycester's Hospital, Warwick, a piece for which a still higher antiquity has been claimed; but 'Anglo-Saxon' it certainly is not. This 'Warwick Chair' has been a good deal reproduced in modern times.

Yet another type of chair much represented by modern examples is the low so-called 'Milking Chair' with a straight narrow back, often pierced with a heart-shaped lifting-hold in its upper part. This type was romantically revived—'revived' is possibly the correct word to use of a kind of chair of which, at the moment, I can recall no veritably antique example—in later Victorian and Edwardian days, often most unsuitably embellished with elaborate carving. But this 'revival' was of the drawing-room order, harmonizing with the potted ferns, silver-framed photographs and other concomitants of a frilly age.

Before quitting the theme of chairs in general, there is a hybrid which should at least be mentioned—the combined Chair-Table. This is the Chair (or Bench, or Settle) with a movable back which, when pulled forward to a horizontal position and secured with a wooden peg, converts it into a table. Examples are not common, if one excepts modern imitations and reproductions. To some of us nowadays, it does not seem a particularly convenient type, but to those of our ancestors who were accustomed to what Lewis Carroll would have called a 'portmanteau' use of their furniture, it doubtless had its advantages. As with the chest, the Chair-Table was capable of various uses, for (besides its other properties) the seat might be boxed and furnished with a lid.

Being quite in accord with the medieval idea, the Chair-Table was doubtless a more or less familiar object in the Middle Ages. The earliest surviving example of it known to me is that illustrated in Plate XXV of my father's *History of Oak Furniture* (1920). Its *provenance* is unknown before it turned up in an Oxford Street shop when I was a boy. This chair-table is of oak, and dates from the end of the fifteenth century. It is of slab-ended construction, each side being formed of a single plank ; their upper part is shaped to form arm-rests, and their lower front edges buttressed. Lifting-grips are cut in the sides. Front and back of the box-seat are formed of planks passed through accommodating slots in the uprights—a typical method of simple construction in use at the period, and also seen in the so-called 'Chair of St Augustine', formerly in Canterbury Museum, and since returned to its earlier home, the Parish Church of Stanford Bishop, Herefordshire. This is not a Chair-Table, and, with due respect to the saintly tradition attached to it, it seems to me (as it seemed to my father) extremely dubious whether it can be anything like as old as the time of Augustine. Incidentally, it too has, or rather has had, a box-seat. Since, however, it is doubtless a country-made piece of fame and a venerable age—even a rough fifteenth-century chair is worth having!—it merits this passing discussion.

One may disagree with the conclusions reached in James Johnston's little book, *The Finding of St. Augustine's Chair* (1898), but it gives a pleasant enough picture of how the chair was sought out by this sympathetic soul and rescued from almost certain destruction. Thrown out of the church, it would have been broken up for firewood, but was begged by the sexton (who knew it of old) as a garden-seat 'to sit and smoke my pipe in'. There Mr Johnston found it; and when he asked after the old church chest, a true 'dug-out', he found it in the cowhouse, doing duty as a cornbin! So scanty was the esteem in which antiquities were held in the eighteen-fifties, which seem to have been the period of Johnston's pilgrimage of grace to Stanford Bishop.

As to Chair-Tables, the few authentic examples that come the collector's way are most likely to be of seventeenth-century date—in other words well after the Reformation and the Dissolution of the Monasteries. This point is made to demonstrate the absurdity of calling such pieces 'Monks' Benches'. That some such articles may have been used in religious houses before the Great Pillage—and doubtless in secular dwellings as well—in no wise justifies the use of the term in connection with furniture made, in some cases, under the Puritan ascendancy of the Commonwealth.

All the same, and whatever their degree of antiquity, old chair-tables are now far from common, so it is with interest that one notes the appearance of one, which, after having 'stood for several generations in the outhouse of an East Devon cottage', came under the hammer in a local auction. Seemingly, it had been none too well treated. The falling-top (I employ the quotation from a book-review in the *Wiltshire Gazette* of 7th August 1930) had been nailed to the arms, and the lidded box-seat used to hold potatoes.

A collector's peace of mind is not ensured when it is added that this scarce item 'was knocked down to the one and only bidder for the sum of threepence'. One could hardly get such a piece cheaper than that!

6 · Of Settles, Forms and Stools

ABOUT the year 1800 there was pulled down in the still rural suburb of Islington, an old house which had seen better days. Known as Ward's Place, it had been cut up into tenements, after having served as a soap manufactory, a dissenting conventicle, and 'an appendage of the Small-pox Hospital in Cold Bath-fields'. But vestiges of a former splendour still lingered about it. In more spacious times, it had been the property of Sir Robert Ducy, or Ducie, Bart, Lord Mayor of London in 1630, who as Charles I's banker is said to have had £80,000 on the wrong side of his books. Earlier, Ward's Place—or Hunsdon House, as it had been called—is supposed to have been the residence of Elizabeth's cousin, Henry Carey, Lord Hunsdon. Its original creation is attributed to Sir Thomas Lovell, K.G. who had fought for the Tudor at Bosworth, and became Speaker of the Commons and Constable of the Tower; and the arms of Dudley in one of its windows were held to point to Elizabeth's Leicester, or the latter's brother, Ambrose Dudley, the 'good' Earl of Warwick.

There was other painted glass in the windows including a roundel of particular moment to this chapter. Its manner (as shown by an engraving of it in Nelson's *Islington*) suggests that it was a relic from the time of Lovell, who died in retirement in 1524. It was held to represent *The Faithful Steward*, and indeed it gives us a good picture of the characteristic setting of such a functionary in Henry VII's day (Fig. 26).

The scene is one of those 'bed-sitters' so frequently used by our ancestors. Seated on a low box-seated settle with a linenfold-panelled back and a foot-rest, the steward is working at a credence-table with cupboard-space in the body of it—another of those pieces of 'portmanteau' furniture esteemed in medieval and Tudor times. A knopped candlestick is poised on one of the side-uprights of the settle, and on the table-top, besides a small mirror, are books, a knife, pounce-box and divers coins or counters used by the good man in his calculations. In the background is another settle, linenfolded as to the back, but with an arcaded substructure, some sort of a cupboard supporting various utensils, and a canopied bedstead. A clothes-brush hangs on the wall. Such interiors as this must have been frequently found in town and country, merely differing in the extent and quality of their furnishing.

There has been much speculation as to the origin of the settle, many good authorities holding that it represented a development of the chest, which, as we have seen, united seating accommodation with its other functions. Add a back and arms to a chest, and one easily arrives at the box-settle. But where some writers err, at any rate by implication, is in assigning the development to too late a period. Box-settles, as well as those of bench-construction, were known medievally, thus damaging the value of certain otherwise satisfactory diagrams demonstrating the process of development from chest to settle by the use of types of seventeenth-century character!

Again, attractive though it is, I doubt the validity of a *general* application of the theory that, like the settle, the Form arose from the Chest.[27] To some extent, this may well have been so. The similarity of construction between, say, boarded chests and forms of the slab-ended type is noticeable, but that *all* forms so originated calls for more explanation than is likely to be forthcoming.

Benches and settles are each divisible into two fundamental types, the fixed and the independent. Of the fixed type of bench the simplest variety is such as is seen in Fig. 19, which admits us straight away into the atmosphere of a Tudor school. Though arrayed by the sixteenth-century draughtsman in the dress of his own day, the incident illustrates one in the life of William the Bastard's father, Robert the Devil, as given in a manuscript apparently based on Wynkyn de Worde or Pynson.[28] The scene is that in which Robert having gone 'to scole a lytell space', and being very reasonably threatened with a flogging for his graceless-ness, slew his master with a dagger-thrust in the belly. (He was by way of being a troublesome brat.) Quite likely the draughtsman's mind turned to his own schoolroom when he composed the drawing, but the setting is one that might have appeared in buildings of various other uses, including domestic. A fixed bench is against the wall, its utter simplicity serving to contrast such more sophisticated examples as the panelled bench at Crowhurst Place, Surrey, which latter bench belongs to the period of Henry VIII.

Since, however, fixed benches are scarcely collectable, and

independent forms and settles of medieval type are all but unobtainable, we are again brought as near to our own time as the seventeenth century. Few examples will be found to ante-date this period, while many are even later in date. The familiar type of settle with back-panels of raised-centre and shaped-top form, sometimes vaguely 'Gothic' in outline, are assignable to the end of the seventeenth, or, still more probably, to the eighteenth century. Sometimes, they are provided with legs of cabriole type, or roughly recalling the cabriole form, this, in some late examples, being reduced, to economize timber, to a shape but little removed from a bulky edition of the ordinary tapered leg of circular section. Again, in certain cases, a compromise is effected between the settle and the sofa, such pieces, when homogeneous, being of late origin. The plain high-backed settle of farmhouse or alehouse type, sometimes comprehends the function of 'bacon cupboard' and other uses; but the initial idea of such pieces was that of a combined fireside-seat and draught-stop, the latter a decided advantage in the draught-ridden kitchens (Fig. 21). By the use of a tall settle or two, the open-hearthed fireplace could be more or less fenced off as a small room on its own account, glowing with a light and warmth that but feebly penetrated to the murky outer spaces. Contemplating such settles as these, we appreciate the more vividly our ancestors' addiction to wearing their hats, not to mention over-garments, indoors as is seen in so many old prints and paintings. The prevalent male hatlessness of to-day has come about in our own time. In my young days, eccentric fellows who went about without headgear were amusedly referred to as 'members of the hatless brigade'.

The Form, which in Tudor times was frequently of the slab-ended variety, had, by the seventeenth century, acquired the turned legs, often splayed at an angle, of similar type to those used for the joined stools of equivalent period. In the turned-leg type, four legs is the obvious minimum, but there may be more, and in the case of Fig. 20, assigned to the Commonwealth Period, we find no less than ten legs to a nearly 5½-foot stretch; but this is extremely unusual. This form, by the way, has been traced to the neighbourhood of Guildford.

Joined stools, more commonly and less accurately known as 'Joint-Stools', were freely used in the household, and in larger establishments could be stacked, head-to-tail, when not in use, in the space beneath the long tables on the stretchers of which they might rest. The alternative term 'coffin-stool' originated from the detail that stools were sometimes used in churches as bier-supports. But though a relatively small proportion of such pieces may perhaps be so called when sufficient evidence to warrant it is forthcoming, 'coffin-stool' is not a name that should be applied to the domestic article.

Of stools in general, it may again be said that the slab-ended type of construction, as also seen in sundry chests, chairs, etc., is characteristic of many average stools of the late Gothic and Tudor periods. Stools of this type are well worth acquiring, though it is as well to satisfy oneself of their antiquity, before doing so, as apart from honest reproductions, clever imitations have been made, some of them from old boarded chests of little consequence. But it should also be remembered that slab-ended stools of semi-Gothic type were made at quite a late period, as is shown by an interesting pair in Midhurst Parish Church, these being actually dated 1689. The pillared or turned legs which, much earlier than this, had replaced the slab-ends, introduce us to the typical Joined Stool, which is somewhat more readily procurable and which, when authentic, is usually of seventeenth-century date (Fig. 8). There was, many years ago, before joined stools had reached their present high peak of value, a revolting tendency to turn them into 'Jacobean Umbrella-Stands', by the simple process of removing the top and fitting a metal tray to the lower stretchers. One doubts whether anyone would be quite so foolish as to do this now, when even poor examples of stool command prices which would have staggered an earlier generation of collectors. But it should be added that joined stools have also been reproduced and imitated, not without excellence, in modern times.

In Chapter II, we made documentary contact with a 'stoole with a lock', in a will of 1650. This would have been a stool with a lifting lid, disclosing a box-structure in the upper part of the framework (Fig. 22). Such stools are still to be found, though a considerable number of them belong to the 'reproduction' class. I have known such pieces to be called 'Bible-Box Stools', though I am not aware of any warranty for this description. More or less distantly related to such pieces is the Close-Stool or 'Commode' (though the latter term is open to confusion with another very different class of furniture). Close-Stools are separable into two main types, the box-form and the drum-shaped. I have recently seen an old Buckinghamshire drum-shaped Close-Stool, with rather good metal fittings of eighteenth-century date. And I have a near-Regency example of mahogany, square-shaped, mounted on four turned feet, and its lid inset with a square of carpet-work, though this particular specimen is of a kind that might very well have been town-made. It is mentioned here because such late pieces are in a remote degree related to the ordinary box-stools of the seventeenth century, some of the deepest of which may conceivably have served a like function. It is obvious, however, that the average seventeenth-century box-stool was not so employed.

Even so unromantic a class of furniture as the Close-Stool is not without its documentary background. Complaining to Cecil of the sorry state of her youngest daughter, the imprisoned Lady Mary Keyes (born Grey) in 1567, Frances, Duchess of Suffolk indignantly instanced 'such a littel piteous canopy of red sarsnett, as was skant good enough to hang over some secret stool,'[29]—Close- and Secret-Stool having one and the same meaning.

There were, of course, other forms of stool though, perhaps, not many of these can now be definitely assigned to a country origin.

One excepts (among others) the plain three-legged 'Milking Stool'; but though, in its primitive way, this represents a type of considerable antiquity, made in various sizes and used for a variety of purposes, surviving examples seldom appear to be of any great age. I should not care to say that those I have seen were likely to be other than 'Georgian', though it is often difficult to assign such primitive, traditional pieces to a precise period. Of course, I speak of antique examples only, the type having been continued till to-day. It is easily understood that items of such small consequence would not have been preserved after they had grown unserviceable.

When we come to Foot-Stools, I can produce an example of both early type and country origin. This little stool (Fig. 23 *bottom*) turned up in the old Sussex vill of Rye in 1916. I was walking down the sunny length of Watchbell Street, when I saw a child playing with it on a doorstep. Scarce trusting my eyes, I hailed my father who promptly went into action and bought the wreck for a small sum off the child's mother. She said it was very old, and had been made by her grandfather. Experience has led me to believe that, in some circles, 'grandfather' is a synonym for 'ancestor', as being the remotest generation they have a name for. Anyhow, here is a foot-stool of late Gothic shape and construction, and exhibiting every obvious sign of a considerable antiquity. Admittedly, the shaping or arching of the front and back is of a form that became traditional, being traceable on furniture of the seventeenth century and even much later; but the general construction of the stool, with its slab-end slotted through the top, is consistent with an early sixteenth-century date, and, making every allowance for traditional methods, it is difficult to see how the piece could be later than that century.

Placed on top of it in the same illustration is a small foot-stool of late Gothic type, introduced for comparison. Stools of a size to accommodate one foot only are in accord with medieval notions, but this particular example, though made of old wood, is of modern construction. This is readily apparent to a trained eye, but a clinching factor is the presence on the under-side of the top, and in a position not easily got at, of an incised stellate roundel of the sort that an eighteenth-century schoolboy might twiddle out with his compasses on a desk-lid. Whether or not this diminutive stool was made to deceive, or merely as a reproduction, is immaterial. It is figured here as a warning to those who might very well buy such a piece for their cottage in the vain belief that they had chanced on a rarity.

7 · Of Tables

MY old friend Charles R. Beard, whose encyclopaedic knowledge of antiquities is accompanied by a first-rate understanding of their 'human' aspects, once committed himself to a diverting reference (I quote from memory) to tables on or under which Oliver Cromwell is said to have slept. Admittedly, we have Pickwickian evidence of the cobbler in the Fleet Prison who slept under a deal table because it reminded him of a four-poster; and a table was held to provide better cover than none against the bombing attacks in 1940 and subsequent years.

But on all such subsidiary uses of the table, whether protective or —to our forefathers—of bibulous connotation, this is not the proper place to linger. We have already seen that other furniture might supply an efficient substitute for the table-top. Here let us concentrate simply on tables as such, with special reference to the more collectable 'country' items.

This at once rules out anything much before the seventeenth century. Early tables were often of the independent-topped variety, so that the familiar trestle-table of modern commercial usage boasts a long and even princely pedigree; but medieval tables of any sort are so extremely rare as to be negligible so far as the ruck of collectors are concerned. Nor is the situation much easier when we come to the great 'melon-bulbed' tables so characteristic of Elizabeth's reign. Of these, genuine examples, especially when of fine quality, are not only rich man's wares, but have been so much imitated and reproduced as to make one cautious even when inspecting certain highly priced items. Even more or less ordinary tables of seventeenth-century date command their price, these usually exhibiting the turned or pillared leg, though some retain the bulbous form in a manner less extravagant than that of the bloated supports at the height of their Elizabethan vogue.

It is important for the beginner to bear in mind that not all antique bulb-legged draw-tables are necessarily Elizabethan or even English. Quite a quantity of Dutch and German pieces have been brought into England, and these, when old, are mostly of seventeenth-century date. With a little experience it is soon easy to distinguish between their shaped bulbs and the sturdier outline of the English pieces.

So far, I have been talking mainly of those Long Tables to which modern collecting has given the unhappy name of 'Refectory Table' (Fig. 24). The intelligent student has only to reflect on the odds against any obtainable table ever having been in a monkish Refectory, to appreciate the undesirability of the label—a mere case of picturesqueness for picturesqueness' sake. Such were the 'oak tables to eat on, long, strong, and well supplied with joint stools,' which Cobbett saw in a Surrey farmhouse in 1825. But there were smaller tables too, of the ordinary dining-, occasional, or side-table varieties, and it is with such as these that the cottage, with its more limited accommodation, would be equipped. Among the side-tables are those bow- or bay-fronted types, often with a flap, of which the less sophisticated examples may in some cases be attributed with confidence to a country origin. It is at any rate partly from tables of this formation that was evolved the familiar gate-legged type, examples of which are seldom earlier than the second half of the seventeenth century.

The appropriateness of the Gate-leg table to a cottage or small country-home is too obvious to need much in the way of comment (Fig. 27). The mere fact that, when out of action, it can be folded and stowed against a wall is a strong point in its favour. Indeed, it is supposed that some very small examples were actually intended for travelling purposes, to eke out the scanty furniture in inns, etc.; in much the same spirit that pairs of travelling candlesticks of brass were made in the eighteenth century and later, with nozzles and cups that screwed together into a metal 'bun' of pocket-size. Very small 'gate-legs' are rare. I have one myself, that can be folded flat, its oval top falling forward like a sort of shield before the undercarriage; and such a seventeenth-century piece certainly could have been used 'on the road'. But 'gate-legs' were made in various sizes, and one large example known to me, from the Honiton district of Devon and now in the possession of my friends Major and Mrs Hugh Giffard, exhibits an unusual feature. Instead of the lower stretchers being plain, as almost always happens, on this table they are carved with lunette-pattern, and I am fully satisfied that this ornament is authentic.

Of later types of table, flapped or otherwise, such familiar eighteenth-century forms as that with the tapered leg, the club- or bun-foot, or that with the cabriole leg, will be among those following accepted patterns, their common characteristic being the use of oak or other, by then, unfashionable woods in place of such more modish materials as walnut, mahogany or satinwood, and perhaps in a simplification of the more elaborate details. It is scarcely necessary to say much about these as, within a little, they follow the normal progression of styles such as may be followed in any general account of antique furniture.

It must not be forgotten, however, that throughout there also existed a mass of very plain tables (and for that matter benches and stools) consisting of no more than a board on roughly shaped supports, such as is frequently represented in the work of Pieter Bruegel the elder and other interpreters of the more boorish side of country life. Such pieces are still made to-day, thus perpetuating a traditional method far older than Bruegel (died 1569), though most of the earlier examples have long since perished, simply because it was worth nobody's while to preserve them. Nor is it by any means easy to 'date' some of the old or oldish examples which may be encountered. A very rough piece which has had hard usage and weathering may be nothing like as ancient as at first sight appears.

A distinction must be drawn between such as these and a mass of very plain, but often well constructed and finished tables of three-or four-legged type, frequently with circular tops, and of eighteenth- or early nineteenth-century date. Indeed, some of them may be later than that. In this class we find such plain, but in its way satisfying, furniture as the 'Cricket Table', a plain three-legged affair so-called from some fancied resemblance to cricket stumps—or, perhaps also, as the earliest cricket stumps were two, not three, in number, from the tables used by the notchers, or to carry the drink-mugs. In any case, 'Cricket Table' is merely collectors' jargon of no validity. Such honest-to-goodness pieces as these and similar tables, dependent wholly on their functional utility, united with the appeal of good wood and a pleasant outline, are usually of late period—say, at the earliest eighteenth century—though it need not be doubted that their ancestry goes back a long way further. It is only in relatively recent times that such plain tables have been thought at all worthy of the collector's notice, which means that very large quantities of them must have fallen to decay or been broken up as worthless. Whatever fancy names we choose to give to them, it is clear enough that such plain tables were used for any necessary purpose in thousands of small homes in town and country.

Mention should be made here of the specialized form of stand which supported the lacemaker's pillow with its dangling bobbins; but, though old examples of these 'horses' occur, they are usually of late period and seldom of much interest apart from the craft practised on them. Of that village craft, now largely supplanted by imported or machine-made lace, one cannot speak without respectful amazement at the skill of those workers who, in many cases, devoted a lifetime to its prosecution. Though local manufacture has sadly declined, there are to this day folk in Buckinghamshire, formerly one of the great rural centres of lacemaking, who can prove their ability at the pillow. In December, 1947, the *Bucks Herald* noted the death, at Leighton Buzzard, of a Mrs M. A. Cox, at the age of 88 years. A native of Padbury, Mrs Cox commenced lacemaking when six years old. Before her removal to Leighton Buzzard in 1917, she lived at Steeple Claydon, and, according to the *Bucks Herald*, she had, at the time of her death, 'over 200 different designs in her possession'. Examples of the bobbins used by such craftswomen as this are still obtainable, some of the older types being interestingly decorated and even inlaid in the manner of 'folk craft'; but there is a world of difference between bobbins lying dead in a glass case, and the same implements when flickered by nimble fingers in the intricate performance of the lacemaking ritual. And from that we return to more usual varieties of household furniture.

One type of table much in demand is the small tripod with turned support and spreading feet (Fig. 30). Such tables are the humble cousins of the splendid 'town' tripods, with claw feet and 'pie-crust' edging which have received so much of the fakers' attention. The mass of plainer, less frilly tripods, a proportion of which were doubtless country-made, are attributable to rather late in the eighteenth century, when they do not belong to the first thirty years or so of the nineteenth. Indeed a great many tripods are of nineteenth-century date, some being even later than the indicated limit; but Victorian tripods readily 'give themselves away'.

In mentioning the small tripod, one should not omit all reference to its larger relative, the circular Dining Table—another convenient type. This also hangs-over well into the nineteenth century, but Victorian tables of whatever shape have not yet been promoted to the antique category, and, though many of them are well made, they are not often conspicuous for beauty.

But (to be platitudinous) distance lends enchantment. Just as our more refined ancestors could not abide the 'barbarous Gothic', so we in our turn have discarded things which our descendants will learn to admire. One only hopes that a machine- and atom-age will leave them something worth looking at!

8 · Of Cupboards, Dressers and Presses

G. K. CHESTERTON once said of a very different subject that it might be written about in one of three ways; of these the third 'would be the most difficult if the other two were not impossible'.[30] It is in a like mood that I approach the present chapter. If the definition of 'chest' and 'coffer' is not as clear as it might be, the situation is no clearer in respect of certain forms of cupboard. For simplicity's sake, I am not attempting, either here or anywhere else in this book, to give all the technical terms with which furniture-studies are so liberally bristled. All of them are important to advanced students; but advanced students can be safely left to look after their own interests. My purpose is merely to deal with such matters as are likely to be useful to the average collector. If, in the cause of a reasonable simplification, I fail to mention this or that term, it need not be taken for granted that I have never heard of it.

First, then, let us come to some understanding of what we really mean by the word 'cupboard', since in modern usage it has swallowed up a number of more specific terms, and is now freely applied to all manner of structures enclosed by doors. When the modern housewife, in search of accommodation, echoes Ann Kipps's wish for 'cubbuds', she usually implies something different from what our earlier ancestors would have understood by that word.

Primarily, the Cupboard was the cup-board—a sort of dresser for the lodgment or display of cups and plate. It had no essential association with doors. But that predilection for 'portmanteau' furniture, previously noted, tended to utilize available space by the provision of a doored compartment, in which various things could be kept. Such enclosed space grew, in some cases swallowing up most or all of the interior parts. Thus, in time, things like the fitted structures with doors in our bedrooms acquired the name of 'cupboard', though in fact they may not be entitled to the term.

Many such fitted 'cupboards' as these are really descended from the old Press, or (if you must have it so) Wardrobe, though the former is preferable as having the wider significance. Wardrobe (in this sense) is properly a press for the safe keeping of clothes. A Press might be used to keep almost anything. A good many of the things we should now vaguely call 'cupboards' were anciently known as Hutches; and cupboards themselves were differentiated in sundry ways. In respect of these, the collector is constantly faced with two terms: Livery Cupboard and Court Cupboard.

To a beginner, my advice about the term 'Livery Cupboard' is not to use it at all. In the whole range of furniture-studies, no term has been more freely misused. Even in publications of a weighty order, it has been completely misapplied. If you must use it, banish the false idea that it has any essential association with uniforms or that sort of livery. Put at its simplest, the Livery Cupboard was a *delivery cupboard*: a sort of dumb-waiter on which plate was displayed and from which food and drink were dispensed to the table (Fig. 31). Its sixteenth-century characteristic is clearly defined in the Contracts for Hengrave Hall, Suffolk, of 1537-38, which tell us (I modernize the spelling) that certain 'cupboards be made the fashion of livery, that is, without doors'. There is no need to go beyond this: a Livery Cupboard was *not* a doored structure whatever anyone may urge to the contrary. In that case, what was it? Presumably, we can recognize something of the sort in George Cavendish's *Life and Death of Thomas Wolsey* when he speaks of, at Hampton Court Palace, 'a cupboard . . . of six desks high, full of gilt plate, very sumptuous'. This seems to have been a super-form of the open, staged structure (otherwise the Buffet or Sideboard or, in appropriate formations, the Dresser), and the fixed, open stands for plate as used by some of the City Companies. The doorless variety of Corner Cupboard and even certain open-fronted Dole Cupboards edge their way in as collateral relations. Some, at any rate, of these various things meet the broad requirements of the Hengrave Hall description, though certain of them are but descendants of the old idea and would not have been known by the name of Livery Cupboard. But if such was the 'livery' type, what was the Court Cupboard?

In general usage nowadays, 'Court Cupboard' is applied to those cabinets with doors under, and a slightly recessed doored-and-panelled upper stage. Of this, the top was supported by carved or turned supports, which later gave way to a mere pendant (Fig. 33). On the other hand, Mr R. W. Symonds (researches conducted by whom have yielded many valuable results) adduced pictorial evidence to show that the term 'Court Cupboard' was applied to completely doorless structures of the 'Buffet' or dumb-waiter type (Fig. 31), such as would have agreed with the Hengrave Hall definition of Livery Cupboard, though one example has a small enclosure, fronted with a door, in the centre of its upper stage.[31] That being so, it is easily understood how more fully enclosed pieces were, or became, known as 'Court Cupboards'. Indeed, I would not go so far as to scout the term in respect of all such pieces, though Mr Symonds prefers to call the like of them 'Press-Cupboards', a good old, if somewhat eclipsed, word doubtless properly applicable to many of them. They are, in effect, the descendants of what in the inventories of Henry VIII's furniture were described as 'cuppbordes wyth ambries', this simply implying a *cup-board* fitted with enclosed and doored compartments, the latter having since usurped the name of 'cupboards'.

If I do not illustrate English examples of these 'Court-' or 'Press-Cupboards', it is because later kinds are figured in so many books on furniture, and also because the less widely known Welsh varieties are their near relatives.

To this class of furniture, then, belong the *Deuddarn* and the *Tridarn* of Wales, so-called according to whether they are two- or three-tiered. The average *Deuddarn* resembles an English Press-Cupboard in all but minor details and a certain national savour more easily recognized in being than defined in words. In some cases, the third and uppermost tier of the *Tridarn* was an addition to the original structure, made, it is said, in accordance with local custom, though some I have seen did not impress me as being particularly genuine. It must be remembered, however, that the furniture of the Welsh countryside was essentially conservative in tradition, and some pieces nominally seventeenth-century in character may actually belong to a much later date. There is a parallel to this in the intense conservatism of Breton carving; but, confining ourselves to little Wales, it is interesting to note by way of example a plain *Deuddarn*, with raised-centre panels, the uppermost with quasi-Gothic tops, which on type might have been assigned to somewhere about the beginning of the eighteenth century (Fig. 33). It, however, bore the initial D and date 1769 in brass-headed nails, and there is no cause to doubt that 1769 was the approximate period of this 'Queen Anne' type of piece. As might be expected, examination showed that there was originally more than one initial, in this case I D. My friend and colleague on memorable occasions, J. R. Fawcett Thompson, who investigated the matter,[32] was able to ascertain the tradition of the piece from its owner. Family tradition is strong in Wales, and there is nothing to militate against this particular instance of it. The *Deuddarn* was said to have belonged to a certain Ioan (John) Daniel, whose daughter married one David Edwards, their descendant in the distaff line being the owner of the piece in 1927. Now David Edwards had the bright idea of changing the initials I D to his own, by the simple process of picking out the nails forming the I, and inserting an E in the sufficient space between the D and the date. But Mr Edwards, having erased the one initial, failed to add the other. He, 'it is said, enjoyed a reputation among his friends for starting a job but never finishing it.' Tradition is often an unsure guide, but this at least covers the obvious facts.

Commenting on Mr Thompson's discovery, my father observed in *The Connoisseur* that 'while I have encountered two-tier cupboards which had probably been deprived of a third storey, I have also found many . . . of which the topmost stage was clearly a modern excrescence. Furthermore, I have had a strong suspicion that sundry small tables of antique fashion were nothing more than the dismantled third tiers of *tridarns*.' He was 'speaking of what was done before collecting reached its present heights—but that the unstable construction of the third tier afforded many opportunities for such offences needs no explanation'.[33] It is indeed certain that, whenever it may have been done in particular cases, *deuddarns* were made into *tridarns* by the addition of a top-tier or canopy, but this does not mean that *tridarns* were never specifically constructed as such, as an integrated three-tier design. A distinguished authority on the Folk Life of Wales, Dr Iorwerth C. Peate, F.S.A., has kindly confirmed for me that 'there are examples of *tridarns* which are completely homogeneous'.

An interesting *Tridarn*, to which Dr Iorwerth Peate has referred me, is in the collection of Colonel J. C. Wynne Finch, of Voelas. It is inscribed and dated 1689 on the canopy, and this doubtless represents the approximate period of the piece as a whole. The lower stages resemble a Press-Cupboard of the latter part of the seventeenth century, with pendants instead of turned supports to the recessed part, and with a generally traditional appearance, heightened by an arcaded centre-panel and a strip of inlay, both of a sort inherited from the early part of the century. It is noticeable that the sides of the third tier are enclosed with flat, unperforated balusters of a late seventeenth-century type anticipating the familiar vase-splats of the earlier part of the eighteenth. I should like to add that in mentioning this and one or two other kinds of Welsh furniture in a book on the English product, I do so for comparative purposes and with no more intent of belittling the Cymric sense of nationhood than of belittling my own. (Fig. 32.)

Another type of 'cupboard' much used in country districts, though certainly not confined to them, was the 'Food-Hutch' (Fig. 34). This is recognizable by its perforated ornament or, later, by its panels pierced with small holes, disposed in patterns, to admit a current of air to the receptacle. Such hutches are ancestral to the modern 'larder-cupboard', with its wire-gauze or perforated metal fittings ; and that many of the old hutches were actually used to hold food-stuffs need not be doubted. That all hutches with perforated ornament were so used is, perhaps, less certain. Most of us have known, by bitter experience, the desirability of having ventilation holes pierced in the fitted 'cupboards' in our bedrooms or domestic offices, to counteract damp and mould, and it may be presumed that our ancestors were no less alive to the necessity of such a manœuvre in rooms with cold, stone-flagged floors. Of perforated hutches, the earliest obtainable are usually of late fifteenth- early sixteenth-century date, but these are rare, sought-after, and a good deal reproduced. Of the later hutches, pierced with diamond or other patterns, many belong to the seventeenth century.

The Food-Hutch is, however, but a single variety of Hutch, a very characteristic form of which was a rather low enclosed structure with doors, about midway between a table and what we now call a 'cupboard'. That in fact such pieces could and did serve a dual purpose, is shown by Fig. 26, where one of them is seen in actual use by an early sixteenth-century steward. The Credence of modern ecclesiastical furnishing—a side-table for the Elements prior to their Consecration—is often based on the same type, for which there is good medieval precedent. Indeed the term Credence is often used of pieces of secular usage.

'Hutch' is an anglicism for the French *huche*, meaning a kneading-trough or meal-tub, though its older significance was wider. Indeed, in A. Ramsay's edition of the *Paston Letters* (1840), *huche* is defined as a 'coffer or chest standing upon legs', though something more in the nature of a doored structure (*e.g.* of 'cupboard-table' type) would seem to be indicated. It need not be supposed, however, that the term was narrowly restricted to such pieces. Our extant term 'rabbit-hutch' indicates the variability of the type, the ultimate meaning of 'hutch' being possibly no more than something in which articles were kept or guarded. In the Paston letter concerned, we read over date October 28th, 1455, how the Lancastrian 5th Earl of Devon's son, Thomas Courtenay, raided 'Radford's Place' at Poghill near Kyrton in Devon, when his retinue robbed Nicholas Radford's chamber and 'rifled his hutches'. That Courtenay (later 6th Earl) was to redden the Rose with his own life's blood, less than six years afterwards, may have warmed poor Radford's ghost though it could mend neither the old man's hutches nor his slit weasand.

Of English hutches of the legged variety the most celebrated is the very remarkable example at St. James' Church, Louth, Lincolnshire, still known by its ancient name of 'Sudbury's Hutch'. This was given to the church by a former vicar, one Thomas Sudbury, whose incumbency began in 1461 and closed with his death in 1504, these dates corresponding with the late fifteenth-century character of the piece. The period is further narrowed by the hutch being carved with heads of Henry VII and his Queen, Elizabeth of York, the Tudor's profile being recognizable. Between them is the Royal Badge of a crowned rose with supporters. All this is good enough, but that the title of Sudbury's Hutch is no archaicism is proved by the earliest specific allusion to it discovered by R. W. Goulding in the church accounts, this being under the year 1586, though by then the hutch must have been almost a century old.

Pieces like this are unobtainable, but the fact that more than one imitation or reproduction of Sudbury's Hutch has been noted, renders some mention of it desirable.

Smaller varieties of 'cupboard', within the collector's reach, include the 'Spice Cupboard' and that popular and useful adjunct the Corner Cupboard (Figs. 38, 39 and 40). Though by no means limited to 'cottage' use, the corner cupboard of its nature was, and still is, particularly serviceable in small dwellings enforcing an economical treatment of space. These pieces were made in various sizes, from small to large, but it is seldom possible to secure anything of earlier period than the eighteenth century. In most cases, the front elevation is flat and most probably panelled, but bow-fronted examples of latish date, sometimes painted, sometimes of a wood such as mahogany, are also found. Occasionally the painted bow-fronts are attributed to such hands as that of Rubens—a fable which may be discounted, but which may have arisen through some of their subjects having been borrowed at second- or third-hand from works of Old Masters.

'Spice-Cupboards', small rectangular pieces, provided with a door and fitted with drawers, owe their name to the probable supposition that many of them held herbs and simples. They could also have been used for a variety of other purposes, though some of the smaller corner cupboards may have served a similar function. Such pieces were, in effect, the medicine-chests of our forefathers' domestic economy. Obtainable examples of spice-cupboard usually date from the second half of the seventeenth century, or later.

In considering these various matters, we have lost sight of the Dresser on the one hand, and the Press on the other. Dressers are separable into two basic types, the low (related sometimes to the Hutch, sometimes to the Side-Table) and the tall (Figs. 35 and 36). Quite early examples are virtually unobtainable, and some of the towering medieval types, as represented in museums, are not wholly authentic. Indeed, any dresser of medieval appearance should be closely scrutinized as such things were a favourite exercise of the nineteenth-century faker. As already suggested, it is within the bounds of possibility that some forms of dresser approximate to the much-discussed 'Livery Cupboard'; but the collector who secures any sort of a dresser of a date prior to the reign of the second Charles is to be congratulated. Dressers of the restored Monarchy are apt to be of side-table type, with drawers faced with ornamentally disposed mouldings. Such pieces did not cease to be made when Charles apologized for being so unconscionably long a-dying, and not a few of such as occur have undergone what may be charitably called 'restoration'. The tall-backed Dresser with shelving (and sometimes with doored compartments) is most usually procurable in examples dating from the end of the seventeenth century, though the majority belong to the eighteenth or even later.

These remarks apply equally to the much-vaunted Welsh Dressers, commenting on which in the original issue of his *Chats on Cottage and Farmhouse Furniture* (1912; p.133), the late Arthur Hayden discouraged a tendency to talk of them 'as though they were a type absolutely apart from any other'. This is true enough; a tall-backed dresser is a tall-backed dresser anywhere, and constructionally the Welsh variety has much in common with the English. All the same, not even the most *blasé* collector will deny a racial individuality to the Welsh product, or a certain tendency to local characteristics within that scope. It is scarcely necessary to illustrate an English high-backed dresser, but a fine example of the 'South Wales' type (which differs in sundry particulars from the 'North Wales') is seen in Fig. 36. Belonging to the Rev. J. F. W. Leigh, M.A., F.Z.S., it is assigned to *circa* 1770 and shows characteristic pierced apron-work. The Welsh Folk Museum has a somewhat similar dresser, though plainer and without pierced work, of early nineteenth-century date from the Swansea Valley. On both examples, the arching of the aprons is almost 'Queen Anne' in type.

A clergyman of my acquaintance has a pleasant example of what he calls a 'Shrewsbury Dresser', because he bought it in that border-town. It is a late type with doored compartments as well as the open shelving in the back. As such, it approximates to the 'North Wales' type of dresser, which (in all the examples seen by Dr Iorwerth Peate, to whom I am much indebted for his advice on Welsh furniture) has an under-stage with drawers and doored compartments, and generally long narrow 'cupboards' on each side of the top stage. It must be added that 'cupboards' and drawers are also found on English dressers.

It is to the tall-backed dresser, wherever made, that is related the ordinary fitted dresser so familiar in kitchens.

Antique dresser-backs, either actually independent or reared on a substructure, are also found. In addition, hanging shelves of various sizes occur, some of which may conceivably have fulfilled a similar purpose. One example (W. 86—1926) in the Victoria and Albert Museum is dated 1655, but it seems to me open to question whether it has not been built-up from previously unrelated fragments, notably a piece of seventeenth-century arcading enriched with tulip- and jewel-ornament. Some other examples of more or less similar type and equally flimsy construction have not altogether convinced me. There can be no doubt, however, as to a small set of hanging shelves in my own collection (Fig. 37). Boldly carved with initials H M and 1713, this piece was discovered by the famous animal painter, Thomas Blinks, on the Hertfordshire border of Essex, and 'the husbandman from whom it was bought termed this relic his candle-box'.[34] Such was doubtless the use to which the good man put it, but the shelves are different from the more usual types of lidded candlebox. At some time, the shelves had been backed with a large seventeenth-century panel, boldly carved with tulip- and diamond-pattern, but this was obviously an interpolation with re-used material. Incidentally, the floor of the uppermost shelf retains piercings showing that it had been cut (doubtless when the shelves were made) from a 'diamond' panel of a seventeenth-century food-hutch.

As to the Press, this tall, enclosed structure is recognizably the direct ancestor of the Wardrobe as is familiar in later and, indeed, modern times. The appearance of fifteenth-century examples (to take them no earlier) is sufficiently known from such pieces as the Almery in York Cathedral, or from the mutilated remains of a less ornate Press in the Parish Church of St. Mary-the-Virgin at Aylesbury. About 1500, we find presses, in character and sometimes in the presence of perforated ornament, suggestive of the hutches of equivalent period. Under Henry VIII, large presses, the fronts panelled with 'Romayne work', the sides with linenfold, were much esteemed, but none of these things comes the way of the small collector, whose chances of acquiring anything earlier than one of the panelled or 'wainscot' presses of seventeenth-century date are virtually *nil*.

Of later Presses, there is no need to speak; they declare themselves unmistakably. But that the subject is not without its romantic side is evidenced by various anecdotes, not forgetting old Jack Bamber's tale of a 'great lumbering wooden press for papers, with large glass doors, and a green curtain inside'. That press in chambers had its ghost—'a pale and emaciated figure in soiled and worn apparel,' which stood erect in it, as nobody who knows his *Pickwick Papers* needs reminding. For that matter, other furniture has been reputedly haunted, though the mass of collections would seem to be wholly immune from that sort of nuisance! Rot and the 'worm' are much more to be dreaded.

9 · Of Beds, Bureaux and Bookcases

(And Chests-of-Drawers—and Things)

GENTLY sounding the same note as that on which the last chapter was ended, we may agree that we have also heard tell of such things as 'haunted' bedsteads. But so far as the present deponent is concerned it is very much a matter of hearsay. When one reflects that, theoretically, it should be as easy to own a haunted soup-plate as a haunted bedstead, it is readily apparent that a person likely to be swayed by such considerations has but little chance of becoming a profound student of the antique. Collectors (not to say students) are made of sterner stuff. One recalls the device adopted by that redoubtable Vicar of Morwenstow, the Rev. R. S. Hawker, to obtain a fine antique bedstead which its rural owner was unwilling to sell. Grimly the Vicar reminded him of the generations of corpses that must have been laid out on that bedstead, painting his word-picture with such horrific details that the owner gladly parted with the venerable relic. It is very noticeable, however, that the Rev. R. S. Hawker was himself in no wise perturbed, and saw no objection to making a 'good buy' by the use of the merest generalization. Every collection of antique furniture includes pieces that may very well have witnessed tragedy; and, of weapons, Charles R. Beard has reasonably observed that 'there is probably not a sword nor dagger in any of the great collections that has not at some time played a leading part in some scene of blood. And yet they rest as peacefully in a cabinet as if they were so many Georgian tea-cups.'[35] Truly, collectors may go about their lawful occasions with an easy mind.

In respect of antique bedsteads, the position is further simplified by their considerable scarcity, so far as the earlier periods are concerned. These, whether 'stump', 'posted', or 'box', have largely disappeared or are otherwise inaccessible to the average buyer. A great many must have been broken up in compliance with changing taste, or when the metal bedstead, with its spring mattress, became a *sine-quâ-non* of 'respectability' in the spacious Victorian age. Waifs, in the form of the carved posts or, perhaps, a linenfold-panelled bed-head, may sometimes still be recognized; but, on the whole, the medieval bedstead and the 'Elizabethan' type (actual or so-called) with its great knops, are all but to seek. Indeed, some (though not all) of the examples that still change hands are open to suspicion either as a whole or in part. Some seventeenth-century bedsteads are still procurable, but, for the most part, it is mainly the mahogany four-poster of eighteenth-century or later date that awaits the purchaser.

Cradles, too, have become rather scarce. Undoubtedly many country examples were made of basket-work (as, for that matter, were certain hooded chairs approximating to the 'hall-porter' type), though a proportion of the cradles carved in oak or other wood may be also assigned with confidence to a rural setting. In some cases, cradles are carved with initials and date, the date presumably recording a birth or the year when the cradle was made, and the initials the parents or the baby concerned. It would be an achievement to obtain a cradle of pre-seventeenth century date, and those with raised-centre panels belong either to late in that century or to its successor.

In a few cases, antique cradles are still used to fulfil their proper function, though the introduction of more up-to-date and hygienic conditions has caused others to be relegated to such purposes as log-boxes, or receptacles for the ferns and plants that disenchant certain interiors. Of these subsidiary uses the first is a matter of taste and convenience; the second, an æsthetic anomaly; but neither should be resorted to should it tend to harm the antiquity concerned. In any case, cradles, like other pieces of furniture, should be carefully examined as some give evidence of having been shamefully tampered with in the bad old days of faking.

So far, this book has not been lacking in a certain simple logic. Types of furniture have been discussed in more or less their proper relationship. In this chapter, a departure from the rule has been made. Alliteration apart, there is no special reason for grouping the Bedstead with, say, the Bureau—or for that matter with the Chest-of-Drawers—though admittedly some early bedsteads were made with 'drawers under'. Be that as it may, we can now quit the bedside (in a manner of speaking) and turn to other matters.

As its title implies, the Chest-of-Drawers is a relative of the Chest, and at least in a measure descended from it. This does not mean that the Chest went out and the Chest-of-Drawers came in, for chests continued to be made in abundance long after the more complex form of construction had asserted itself. Articles of furniture formed with a number of drawers are found as early as the sixteenth century, but the main link between the Chest and the Chest-of-Drawers is that type, already known in the same century, of which the lowermost stage was fitted with drawer-space, the upper and more capacious portion being of the usual box-like formation. Add more tiers of drawers, swallowing up the box space, and there is the Chest-of-Drawers as familiar to us. Thus, within a little, we have the development of the piece alternatively known in later times as 'Tallboy' (in America, 'Highboy') or 'Lowboy', according to their stature. As regards pieces of earlier date than these, the collector still has a fairly fruitful field among those with drawer-fronts exhibiting mitred mouldings ornamentally disposed, and which became popular under Charles II, though the style outlived his reign (Fig. 42). Not a few of the Chests-of-Drawers which rather mildly adhere to this mode can more probably be assigned to the somewhat later period loosely known as 'William III', which spreads over into the early years of the eighteenth century. As for the rest, it may be briefly suggested that the mass of country chests-of-drawers, in whatever wood or style, come from one part or another of the hundred years or more which is summed up by the useful label 'Georgian' (Fig. 43).

Take a chest-of-drawers, add to it a desk (see Chapter IV), and the net result is a Bureau. Add to that, again, an enclosed upper structure, and you have the Bureau-Bookcase or Bureau-Cabinet. One speaks here of the sloping-topped variety of Bureau though the fall-front type must not be forgotten. Both have good pedigrees. The slope-top sort is in some sense, if rather tenuously, related to medieval usage, and the Standing Desk in Shakespeare's Birthplace affords an approach to the Bureau of later times. This famous desk is certainly a country piece, and, whether or not it was actually used by the youthful Swan of Avon, its construction is consistent with a sixteenth-century date. As it possesses a deep box-compartment beneath its gentle slope it can be accepted as ancestral to the drawered bureau of the end of the seventeenth century and later. As to the fall-type, sixteenth-century examples are known, though the majority of them are certainly importations from abroad, and it would seem that most were not supplied with stands until a later period. However, by the time of Charles II, the standing fall-front bureau was in existence as a homogeneous unit, and is acceptable as an ancestor of all types of Bureau or Bureau-Bookcase in which the slope is dispensed with in favour of a flat fall-front.

From the practical collector's view-point, it can be accepted that the Bookcase, as such, came into prominence under Charles II, though in fact it has a considerably longer history. Its remoter past, however, was so much bound up with collegiate or ecclesiastical libraries, and the setting of a limited number of erudite scholars, as to be of more moment to antiquaries and students than to collectors concerned with what they can buy. It must not be supposed that this fleeting allusion to early bookcases is in anywise contemptuous; but it was under the Merry Monarch that the domestic history of bookcases may be fairly said to have begun.

For a long while afterwards there would have been but little need for such things in cottages or small country-houses, and if (from about Queen Anne's time) some more or less simple form of Bureau-Bookcase were found therein, it would probably have amply sufficed the average need. On the other hand, the low type of Bookcase which first really attained its long-enduring popularity about the time of the Regency, could also have accommodated any increasing flow of literature into such average rural home as had any use for it.

10 · Of Panelling, Clocks and the rest

PANELLING may or may not be met in old cottages or small country-homes. On the whole it was the simpler forms that found favour there, when they were present at all—for many cottages never knew any such amenity. Exceptions exist to this generalization, though it is sometimes apparent in such cases either that the building has decayed in dignity or that the panelling has been removed from elsewhere after it had fallen from the grace of modishness. No absolute rule can be laid down in such matters, but two examples, both now in the Victoria and Albert Museum, and both of West Country *provenance*, serve to demonstrate the more obvious degrees of status round about 1500. On the one hand, we have a superb hall-screen, originally a possession of the Giffards at the Old Manor House, Brightleigh, North Devon, profusely ornamented with arcading, linenfold, and shields, all doubtless at one time gay with colours. On the other, a plain screen of 'Yeoman's Hall' type, said to have come from a small manor house in Devon or Somerset, and stoutly though rather rudely constructed of heavy uprights forming a framework panelled with planks, and enclosing two doorways through which the service from the buttery was conducted.

Except for a limited amount of seventeenth- and eighteenth-century wall-panelling, however, but little awaits the average buyer, who has mainly to rely on the acquisition of loose panels or fragments. Admittedly loose panels may have come from any one of various sources; chest-fronts, bedheads, cabinets, and the general *detritus* of antiquity; but they are convenient for study and can be arranged on the wall to good effect. I myself have a small collection of such items, including an interesting array of linenfold of various kinds, English, French and German. And it is in the form of loose panels, or short 'runs' of panels, that the collector of modest means has the best chance of indulging his or her taste for the once popular but now rare 'Romayne work', of which the principal characteristic is the heads in roundels so favoured in the time of Bluff King Hal (Fig. 48). Occasionally these heads belong to the sphere of actual or intended portraiture, though the majority are formal. Various other types of panel, from medieval to much later times, await the collector, as well as those terminal figures, part human, part architectural, freely known as 'caryatids', of which some of the less sophisticated types have all the air of being by rural carvers. Caryatids (Fig. 49; 'Atlantes' is the preferable term for male figures) are so-called in allusion to the ancient legend of the women of Carya,[9] and represent a Renaissance revival of the form seen at its most famous in the supporting figures of the Erechtheion at Athens, one of which can be studied, nearer home, in the British Museum.

At one time, almost any piece of English furniture (chests, bedsteads, 'court cupboards', etc.) bearing caryatids was pretty well sure to be labelled 'Elizabethan', though it is now known that their use long outstripped the reign of the Virgin Queen, surviving into Charles I's time, and, as a crude provincialism, even well into the latter half of the seventeenth century. It is also possible that there is some relationship between these figures and the heads on the 'Mortuary Chairs' discussed in Chapter V.

But whether panels, to return to them, are medieval, Tudor, or such as the 'diamond', 'tulip', or other types of the seventeenth century, it is a mistake to ignore them merely because they have been separated from their original structure. Not infrequently they afford the collector an opportunity to acquire examples of rarities completely outside his reach in their entirety.

Among other items of furniture not so far noticed should be briefly mentioned Spinning-Wheels, Bellows and Clocks. They are unrelated, for if the Spinning-Wheel relates to anything it is, by its supporting structure, rather to the Stool. To a great extent the old foot-operated Spinning-Wheel has lapsed from use, and its antique forms are merely picturesque survivals. Obtainable examples rarely ante-date the eighteenth century, or at best the latter part of the seventeenth. In passing, one would very much like to know what happened to that spinning-wheel, reputedly found in a blocked-up room at Hampton Court Palace and, again reputedly, worked by the ghostly agency of Edward VI's foster-mother, old Mistress Penn?[36] It is a good, grue tale as Ernest Law tells it: the sounds of whirring and muttering, the unmasking of a walled-up room in which was the spinning-wheel, the flooring beneath it worn away where the treadle had touched it. But how? Was it because the wheel was revolved by a draught from the ivy-grown window, as a correspondent of Mr Philip Lindsay's has stated?[36] For the betterment of the association with Mistress Penn, who was born a Hampden, it is hoped that the spinning-wheel was of her period. With or without a haunting, a Tudor spinning-wheel would be a find indeed!

Of Bellows not much need be said, though they have a long history. Old examples, usually eighteenth- or early nineteenth-century, occur, but most of the extant bellows are modern, though often made in retrospective styles. This applies to many ornately carved pieces of Italianate type, quite a number of which are nineteenth-century copies of Renaissance designs. Old English bellows are normally much plainer. One refers of course to 'squeeze' bellows, though the existence of a late form, in metal, worked by a wheel, should also be noted in passing.

Clocks had but little place in cottage homes before the latter part of the eighteenth century, to which, and to the earlier part of the nineteenth, belong the mass of so-called 'Grandfather Clocks' by country makers. This detail should be appreciated, as inexperienced buyers are apt to rate all antique time-pieces at one and the same level, irrespective of age and quality. With the r[illegible] and valuable town types of clock this book has no concern, whether of the Long-Case (so-called 'Grandfather'), Bracket, or Table varieties. Such pieces as these may have been at ease in Great Houses, furnished from the big towns, but more rarely in lesser settings, and not at all in the homes of the small farmer or the hind. However, the wide array of country clockmakers—even more numerous than the closely packed list in Britten's *Old Clocks and Watches and their Makers* has space to indicate—has left us with a goodly heritage of long-case and bracket clocks: sound, honest, sightly pieces, still capable of serving a useful purpose. I well remember the queer sensation experienced when visiting an author-friend of mine, the late Dr C. J. S. Thompson, and seeing my own surname staring at me from the face of a long-case clock, in his Dining Room. 'Roe, Midhurst' was the inscription. And, sure enough, in the churchyard of that ancient Sussex town are divers mouldering tombstones to the memory of eighteenth-century members of such a family.

As there were many highly-skilled provincial clockmakers, it would be unrealistic to suppose that country-made timepieces, or those intended for the less exalted types of home, were necessarily low-grade. Superior clocks still turn up in country districts, some of them by makers unrecorded in the closely packed pages of Britten; though such as these have but little in common with, say, the so-called 'Cottage Grandfathers'. The latter are often good, serviceable, hard-wearing pieces in cases of unfashionable woods such as oak, and most of them date from the eighteenth or earlier part of the nineteenth century. Sometimes a more ambitious case was attempted for the sake of buyers of more 'towny' tastes, as with Fig. 50, a piece of roughly 1785-90, which has a case mainly of mahogany though the sides of the 'trunk' are of stained oak, thus economizing the more valuable wood.

The dials of 'Cottage Grandfathers' may be of brass, or of painted metal, the latter being sometimes embellished with such decorative devices as a ship or a cottage-scene, these paintings not infrequently showing Dutch influence. Some, again, have the further refinement of a rotating dial giving the phases of the moon, usually shown as a more or less cheerful human face which must have helped to keep alive the ancient epithet 'moon-faced'. These moons may be depicted in a firmament of formalized stars, or alternated with daylight scenes which, if incongruous, add a spice of variety to the clock-face. In Fig. 50, these views are of a lakeside cottage and barn, and a bluish piece of Dutch shipping of attractive colour. The fashion for depicting ships flying the Dutch tricolour had become traditional, its origin going back to the Van de Veldes whom Charles II had imported from Holland, and to whom was largely due the establishment of the British School of Marine Painting. That the provision of moon-dials was more than a pleasant conceit is obvious. In *A History of English Clocks* (King Penguin Books, 1947), Mr R. W. Symonds properly stressed their utility to intending travellers by coach or horse; but, beyond that, the feature was serviceable to farmers and others, not forgetting such superstitious persons as dreaded the ill-luck of glimpsing the new moon through glass. Another detail emphasized by Mr Symonds in the same delightful little book is the difference in the build of North- and South-Country long-case clocks in the late eighteenth-early nineteenth-century, those of Lancashire, Cheshire and Yorkshire tending to be broader and showier than those of more southerly origin, including London. It should be added that ship-paintings on clocks, though far from being confined to the coast, were particularly popular in the neighbourhood of sea-ports.

Among timepieces favoured in latish cottage-homes was the hanging 'Dutch Clock', nakedly exposing its works to the public gaze, as Dickens somewhere noted. Sometimes, such timepieces were fitted with automata, in much the same way as other clocks were supplied with movable moons or shipping. The haymaker gleaning his crop of seconds on the Dutch Clock in *The Cricket on the Hearth* supplies us with another literary allusion to these whimsies. In nineteenth-century country homes of the lesser sort, a type of hanging clock that gained much popularity was that in a glass-fronted case, a part of the glass being under-painted with various kinds of naturalistic or formal ornament. (Fig. 51.)

I am an old Kensingtonian, and I confess that it was not until I settled in Buckinghamshire that I realized that many of these clocks not merely *looked* American, but were in fact of American origin. Happening to see one in a local rectory, I noted the presence of a Connecticut label—Connecticut having a long association with the history of American clockmaking—inside the case. When others were shown to me nearby, I began to sit up and take notice. These nineteenth-century clocks, in wooden cases sometimes displaying split-baluster and other ornament of debased American-Empire design, are well enough known in the United States, and it would seem that they also reached England more or less freely. Mr Desmond Butler, whose professional activities have given him excellent opportunities of studying antique furniture in the Princes Risborough district, has told me that quite a number of these clocks have been found in cottages thereabouts. Some of them—'Improved Thirty Hour Brass Clocks,' the 'brass' presumably referring to the movement only, for the painted faces are usually of another alloy—still bear the printed label of the 'E. N. Welch Mfg. Co., Forestville, Conn., U.S.A.' Presumably some enterprising drummer of the last century 'cleaned up' satisfactorily by vending these blatantly decorated timepieces to the impressionable cottagers of Bucks, and, for all I know to the contrary, of other English counties. When we grumble at the drain of goods to America, we should not forget that the shoe was here on the other foot! But let us return to English-made items.

In certain old country inns, one may still see hanging the huge 'Act of Parliament Clocks', occasioned by Pitt's impost on all clocks and watches in 1797. So unpopular and restrictive was this tax that it was repealed in 1798, but not before various inns and other buildings had installed one large and easily legible clock to compensate for the general disuse of timepieces. Such clocks are usually, though not invariably, coloured black with gold or yellow figures. As relics of a justifiably hated piece of legislation, defeated by the weight of public opinion, Act of Parliament Clocks are worthy of preservation, though they can scarcely be called collectable.

There is, of course, also the time-honoured Hour-Glass or Sand Glass, used in other circumstances than to time prosy preachers' discourses; while a form of timepiece sometimes collected to the buyer's disadvantage is the Water-Clock, which traces its ancestry to the *clepsydra* of remote antiquity. There is not, I think, much evidence to suggest that Water-Clocks were ever extensively used in England. One, in Norwich Castle Museum, has on its wooden hanger a brass tube. This tube, when filled with water, supported a pointer secured to a float, which slowly sank as the fluid ran out of the lower end of the tube. On each side of the pierced recess accommodating the pointer are plates incised with the hours from VI to VI. Other plates bear the names 'Parson' and 'Norwich', and date (in Roman numerals) 1610. In principle, this timepiece is an adaptation of a method known in Ancient Egypt, Greece and Rome; but many English Water-Clocks have no antiquity to recommend them, despite the names and dates they bear. Indeed, some of them boast tubes presenting a strong family likeness to the brass cases of shells as used by modern, or at any rate recent, artillery. Water-Clocks should always be closely examined before they are purchased. An old one is at least interesting; a modern example of quasi-antique workmanship may be an atrocity, its rough and pseudo-primitive character insufficiently cloaking a host of æsthetic and practical sins.

The type of under-painted-glass clock, previously mentioned, and which in its latest and least endurable spasms can be extremely garish, has its counterpart in the ornament of certain Mirrors. It must be premised that reference is solely made to pieces such as might be found in smaller town and country settings, and not to the eighteenth-century elegancies, with inset oil paintings, which command their due price in antique shops. Mirrors for lesser country homes would have been small, and surviving examples are mostly of late period, such as little swing-mirrors (Fig. 43), and the less elaborate wall-types with small balls inset in the moulding of the gilded frame. Dickens, who, apart from his readability, supplies a mine of references to things since become collectable, gives a vivid pen-picture of what had been a fashionable item, but had come down in the world, in his account of the meeting of Mr Jarvis Lorry and Lucie Manette in a room at the 'Royal George' at Dover. He writes of a 'gaunt pier-glass', 'on the frame of which, a hospital procession of Negro Cupids, several headless and all cripples, were offering black baskets of Dead-Sea fruit to black divinities of the feminine gender'. With due respect to Dickens, one rather feels that that mirror could not have been of any age in 1775; but similarly dilapidated pieces of late eighteenth- or early nineteenth-century date not infrequently found their way to settings inconsistent with their shabby vestiges of taste.

On the other hand, the extensive period known to us as 'Regency' coincided with the 'upstart' tendencies among the farming population—tendencies deplored by William Cobbett. Thus it is not at all impossible that a certain amount of fashionable or quasi-modish mirrors may have found their way direct to the lesser country homes.

To enumerate the various kinds of Mirror is unnecessary, but collectors may be advised that a certain amount of eighteenth-century types are 'reproductions'. I have one myself, made in the High Wycombe area whence has emanated so much modern furniture in revived or traditional styles. Its shaped wooden frame closely follows an old model, though the piercings of its arched surmount perhaps lack something of character. It should be added that this, like others of its kind, was openly sold and bought as what it really is—a copy.

Mention of painted mirrors in a previous paragraph suggests the desirability of a few words—and a few words only—on the subject of pictures as such. How one hangs one's walls in this respect is a matter for individual taste, but it can be taken that prior to the photograph- and chromo-infested days of the later Victorian and Edwardian periods, the cottage boasted but little in the pictorial line. Indeed, until the seventeenth century or thereabouts, it would be lucky if it had anything at all, and then perhaps not much more than a print or so, or some broadsides pinned to the wall. Cheap coloured prints or the coarser Glass Pictures of the Harvesting, Sporting, or *Death of Nelson* type belong to the latter part of the eighteenth and the early part of the nineteenth centuries—Nelson, we may remind ourselves, received his mortal hurt in 1805; and the coloured or tinselled Theatrical Portraits commenced, for practical purposes, about the same period, though the main spate of these almost exclusively Cockney products opens in the eighteen-twenties and 'thirties. These latter prints well consort with some of the more histrionic of the pottery figures which continued to erupt from the potteries of Staffordshire and other places for many a long year. Indeed there is a close correspondence between the two media, as in the case of the figures of romanticized Highlanders with short kilts and pneumatic calves, which are clearly related to the same mood that resulted in the 'Scenes and

Characters' of the Juvenile Drama. A realization of this rather obvious fact might have obviated the 'mistaken attribution of the whole class [of the pottery figures] to Scotland, where,' as Mr W. B. Honey tells us in his *English Pottery and Porcelain* (1933, p.231), 'much less clean and pleasant figures were certainly made in the same style'. The truth is that whether these various stage Highlanders—in print or pottery —emanated from London, Staffordshire or Scotland, they represent a popular movement, romantic and even theatrical in origin.

In mentioning Staffordshire figures, I do not allude to the rare and early kinds which are beyond an average beginner's means, but to the more familiar 'cottage ornaments' ranging from the late eighteenth century well into the nineteenth. These, whether human or animal figures and groups, or anything else, are often effective and spirited in their naïve way, and some interestingly reflect the dress and habits of the people. Such of them as were not of (more or less) local invention, were imitated from any handy source, as in the case of that best-known of the groups, *The Tythe Pig*, borrowed from a Chelsea-Derby model. (The point of this satire was that the parents had brought their tenth babe to the bewigged and cassocked parson, in lieu of the tithe pig due to him, and which was less easily spared!) Biblical incidents also occur, and there is a large array of 'portraits' of personages in the public eye, from royalty to Abraham Lincoln and Garibaldi—'Honest Abe' being, shown as a conventionally heroic figure on a wildly improbable but splendidly spirited charger. Such pieces often disclose their period by the identities of the notables concerned, and even some of the latest in date retain a superbly 'primitive' quality. Indeed, certain excellent examples of their kind belong to no earlier than the 1860's, though even these have been faithfully reproduced at a much more recent time. It is extremely dangerous to assume that such cottage ornaments have escaped imitation on the score of their 'cheapness', their present price being much in excess of the modest sums they originally commanded.

Another point about Staffordshire pottery ornaments that may be noted concerns certain dummy clocks, poor relations of the elaborately ornamental time-pieces of expensive homes of a somewhat earlier date. These ornaments with simulated clock-faces and hands were designed to appeal to such as could not afford the real thing for their parlours. In the same way, inferior jugs of 'silver' lustre, or glass candlesticks with a mercury-filling to imitate silver, found their way as Fairings into many a cottage-home.

But pottery (not to say glass) in general is beyond the main scope of this book, whether it be in the form of such traditionalized fancies as *Success to the Plough* mugs; of Willow Pattern (originally of Caughley) or the blue of Spode; of queer little cottages, improbable pink or grey castles, or lop-eared 'Comforter' dogs of a semi-boiled aspect. Be it added again that the wise investor in even such things as nineteenth-century 'comforters' should not buy without caution. These homely deckings of the mantelshelf were made in much the same way for generations on end, and have not escaped reproduction.

This is only too true of the Toby Jug, an eighteenth-century innovation which passed through sundry phases and has multiplied itself to the vexation of inexperienced collectors. The taste for decorating pottery receptacles with human masks, or of actually forming them as human figures, is ancient and recurrent; and it is not unsignificant that the 'Toby' should have made its appearance when the 'Greybeard' or 'Bellarmine' jug—itself a relatively late anthropomorphism—was hopelessly old-fashioned. The 'Greybeard', indeed, had come into fashion in the sixteenth century, was largely produced, though mainly abroad, in the seventeenth (Fig. 52), and continued on into the eighteenth. Equally, the 'Toby' was to pass into folk-lore, though as a more direct symbol of good liquor and good fellowship. Its form purported to show a genial being named 'Toby Philpot' or 'Fillpot', whose mortal clay was made into a jug and that of his wife 'Agnes' into tobacco-pipes; thus ensuring for both a continuance of their earthly harmony. Such is a ballad-maker's tale, though those of us who remember that highwaymen were said to ply the 'High Toby' may see a less happy side of the medal. Though the prime form of Toby Jug is that of a bibulous individual in a tricorn hat and dress to match, some, mostly more recent, types take other shapes including caricaturish portraits of real notabilities. But enough of pottery . . .

For a last word about pictures, let us remind ourselves that though family portraits are now a frequent occurrence in small country homes, their presence there in earlier times—say from the sixteenth century—would have been largely dictated by personal considerations, and the status of the family concerned. The cheaper type of miniature was abroad in the eighteenth century, though the main flood of the Shades or Profiles, which we term Silhouettes, though arising in the same period, belongs rather to the nineteenth. Portraits in oil were provided for the lower or less accessible grades of society by minor practitioners, including itinerant painters who travelled about picking up orders (now termed 'commissions') as they went. Nor were all of these local or itinerant artists contemptible. I have in my Study a good portrait of a male relative, probably done at Ipswich by an unknown working in a Wilkiesque manner, which is good enough to have attracted the attention of distinguished artists. Less excellent, but in its way competent, was another 'Early Victorian' portrait of a most respectable ancestress of the fisherfolk in whose cottage I once stayed on the Essex coast of the Thames estuary. It is a vast mistake to suppose that a proper pride of family is the preserve of the aristocrat or, what is by no means necessarily the same thing, the rich.

Nor, for that matter, should heraldry be regarded as synonymous with snobbism. It may be that a person is genuinely an 'armigerous gent'. It may be that he is descended from a grandfather who (to paraphrase Oswald Barron) optimistically used a 'crest' on his tea-spoons. It may be that he has a more general taste for those pretty cups and saucers, plates and what-not, enamelled with the armorial ensigns of a more elegant age. Or, again, it may be that he relishes a bit of stained glass: say an example or so of those small diamond-shaped panes known as 'Quarries'. In any acceptable form, a touch of heraldry is a grace-note in the home.

If it be argued that such is out-of-place in farmhouse or cottage, my reply is 'Don't you be too sure of that!' The conception of armory as connoting aristocracy or gentility—I say nothing here of arms of rank or office—is of relatively late occurrence, and armorial bearings were more frequently used in non-aristocratic circles than is generally realized. (I can cite offhand the will of a substantial Suffolk yeoman named Owen Danbrook who, in 1619, left to Thomas, son of his cousin Thomas Barnish, his father's seal of arms —*vide Notes and Queries*, 13th October 1923.) Quite apart from that, English families not only have their ups-and-downs, but throughout history you may find a wide variety of rank, status, and financial resource in a single family tree.

To give examples of titled or gentle persons who declined to the poor-house or to a pauper's grave would be unprofitable; but we may at least remind ourselves how certain descendants of a great baronial family, the Suttons or Dudleys, became painters and glaziers, while one, in the earlier part of the nineteenth century, was to be found 'taking toll at a turnpike almost under the very walls of those feudal towers that gave name to the Barony of which he is coheir'.

Sic transit . . .

11 · Of 'Courting Pieces'

(with the Curious Story of Susan Meadows) [37]

IN the year of Grace 1665, His Most Sacred Majesty King Charles II being on the Throne of his forefathers, and the Great Plague raging, a man named Meadows in far-away Suffolk is rumoured to have occupied his leisure in carving a small table-desk for his wife. One says 'wife' because it seems likely that Susan Meadows had already entered the married state; unless Master Meadows, in carving that desk, anticipated the event by giving her the same second initial as his own.

Such is inferred from tradition; but we have the desk itself with its date and its sets of initials and multiplex ornament, among which a round dozen of hearts testifies to a tender occasion (Fig. 45).

I had known of the desk for many years, but never set eyes on it until late in 1945 when it came to me under the will of my distant kinswoman, Miss Amelrosa Cobbold, of Blythburgh, Suffolk. The tradition of the desk had been the subject of correspondence between Miss Cobbold and me, and, back in 1916, J. Seymour Lucas, R.A., F.S.A., that eminent artist and acute connoisseur, had written to my father about it. Not often does the student find so good an opportunity to examine the value of tradition as relating to the lesser sort of country furniture, which is why the matter is here discussed at length to indicate the means whereby other cases may be tested. As will appear, my research brought in data of more than localized interest.

Coincident with the fashionable styles of woodwork, and even with the average less-modish sorts, there existed in the seventeenth century and later what one is tempted to term a 'Third Style', most frequently met with in Treen Ware but also encountered in furniture. At its higher levels, this 'Third Style' resulted in professionally made pieces; at the lower, it shades off into the widespread family of folk-crafts, frequently with a strong implication of home-manufacture. In the unprofessional category we have such things as the Welsh Love-Spoons, made for their sweethearts by ardent swains who enlivened, with such 'spooning', the monotone of many a chaste moment. [38]

Notes on plates, see p. 32

26 *The Faithful Steward :* a bed-sitting room of Henry VII's time

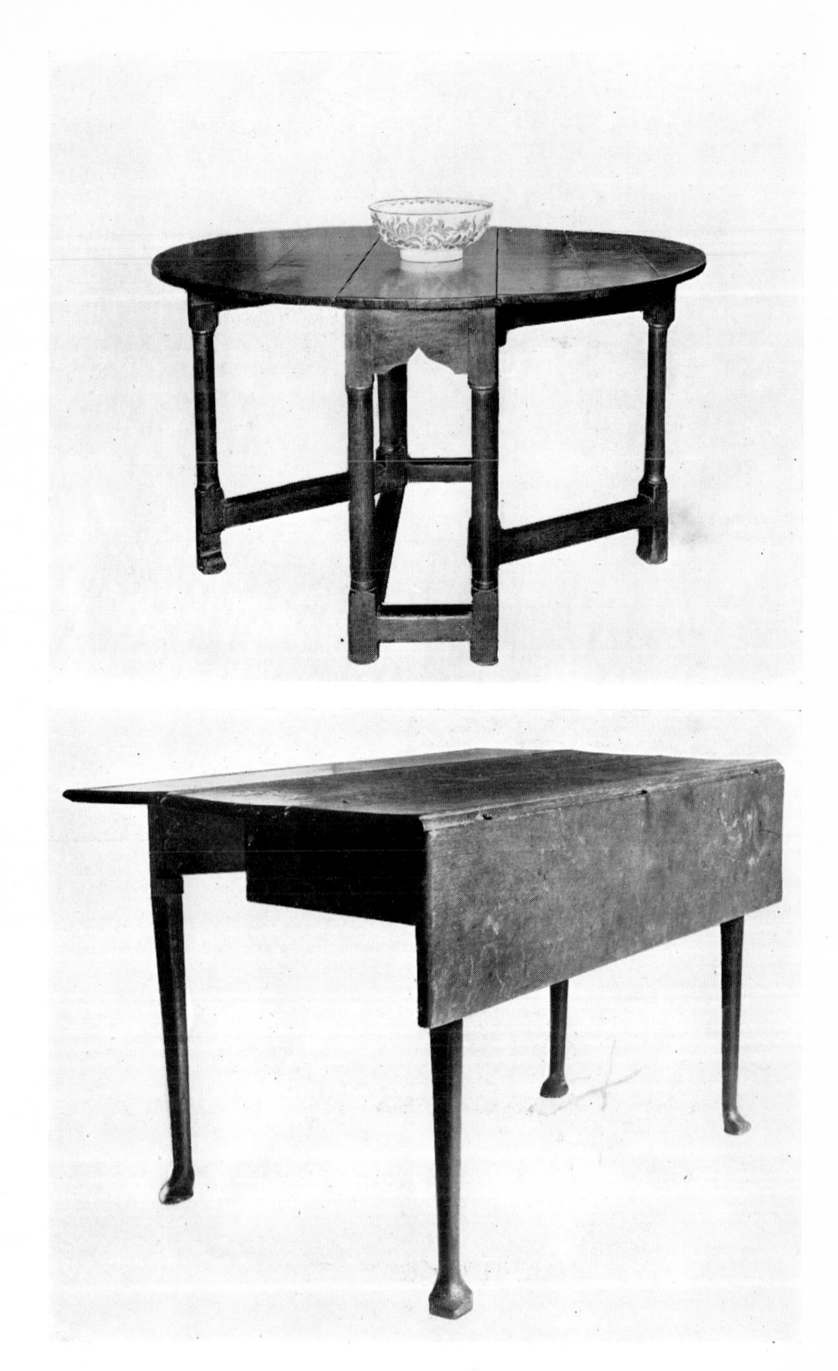

27 *Top* : Gate-leg table, end of seventeenth century **28** *Foot* : Flap-table, eighteenth century

29 *Left :* Semi-traditional table, late eighteenth century **30** *Right :* Tripod-table, early nineteenth century

31 Buffet, first half of seventeenth century

32 *Left* : Welsh tridarn, dated 1689 **33** *Right* : Welsh deuddarn of Ioan [John] Daniel, 1769

34 *Top left :* Food-hutch, first half of seventeenth century **35** *Foot :* Dresser, latter part of seventeenth century **36** *Right :* South Wales dresser, *c.* 1770

37 *Top left :* Hanging shelves, 1713 **38** *Top right :* ' Spice-cupboard ', seventeenth century **39** *Bottom left :* Standing corner-cupboard, eighteenth century **40** *Bottom right :* Hanging corner-cupboard, eighteenth century

41 The Haunted Press in Jack Bamber's story [*Pickwick Papers*]

42 *Left :* Chest-of-drawers, second half of seventeenth century **43** *Centre :* Bow-front chest-of-drawers, late eighteenth century, and a small swing-mirror of early nineteenth-century style **44** *Right :* A deep bureau, junction of the seventeenth and eighteenth centuries

45 Two views of ' Susan Meadows' desk ', 1665

46 Two views of chip-carved box with a love posy, mid-seventeenth century

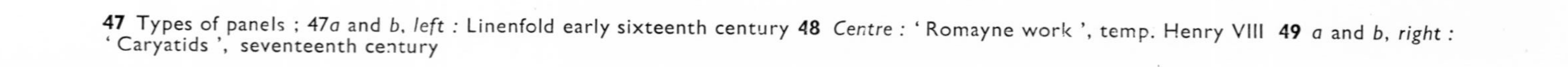

47 Types of panels ; 47*a* and *b*, *left* : Linenfold early sixteenth century **48** *Centre* : ' Romayne work ', temp. Henry VIII **49** *a* and *b*, *right* : ' Caryatids ', seventeenth century

50 Long-case clock, by Richard Cole, Ipswich, late eighteenth century

51 *Right* : American clock, nineteenth century, of a type found in many English cottages

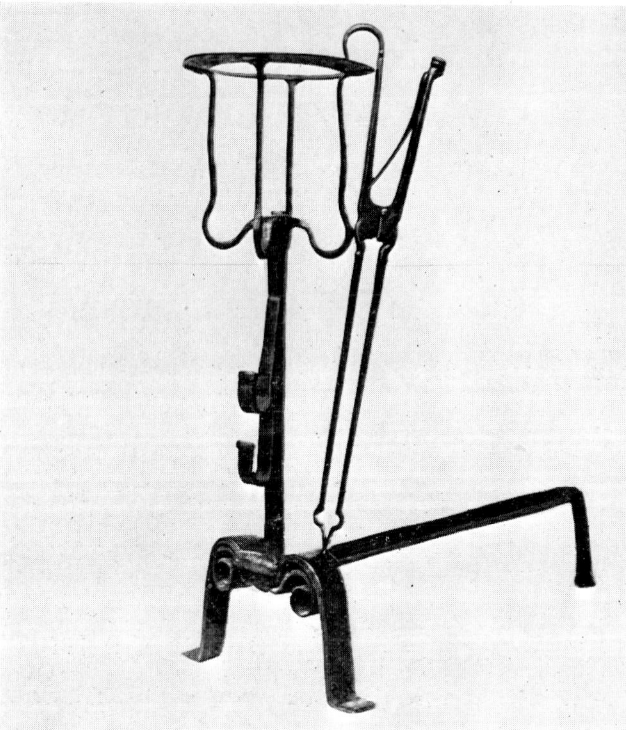

52 *Top :* Rushlight-holder, first half of seventeenth century ; ' Greybeard' jug, 1660; ' shoe ' muller, early nineteenth century **53** *Foot :* Firedog, first half of seventeenth century, and a pair of eighteenth-century ember-tongs

Types of brass candlesticks ; **54** *Top :* late seventeenth-early eighteenth century
55 *Foot :* Some eighteenth-century types of brass canclesticks

56 Armorial stained-glass quarry, seventeenth century: Seckford/Rowe (Roe)

Evidently some rustic swains attempted more ambitious mementoes than these. 'Courting Furniture' would not be a bad term for some of these items, though it must be premised that only a proportion of countrymade stuff of the type can be properly assigned to the 'courting' division.

Of such 'Courting Furniture', 'Susan Meadows' Desk' is a remarkably instructive example. I shall revert to its history later; but something should be said in this place of its physical aspect. Quite small in size—the overall dimensions are about 5½ in. greatest height, by 17 ins. wide, by 12¼ in. deep—it is carved on almost the whole of the front, sides and top with a medley of ornament including hearts (some superimposed with crossed arrows), two *fleurs-de-lys*, a bush of four feathers, acorns, whorls, and flowers, with a device resembling a maze and a quantity of other formal decoration, parts of it so strangely 'Celtic' in aspect as to make one wonder whether the carver had seen some dug-up metal ornament (?). Within, a shelf enclosed by a front pierced with two scrolled openings is neatly if crudely contrived.

Though the whole design is clearly amateurish, it reflects contemporary taste in sundry details. For example, on the front edge of the lid is a small cherub's head; and a carved top-rail or stop, partly intended to keep the lid from being flung too far back and wrenched from its hinges, accords with the exuberant taste of 'Restoration' furniture, so-called in allusion to the Glorious Restoration of King Charles II, and not on account of its having been in any way renovated. Small brass knuckles have replaced the original hinges, and it was doubtless at the same time in the nineteenth century that certain repairs were made to the woodwork.

Most important are the two sets of initials and the date on the slope. I confess that so unusual, not to say inconvenient a feature as the overall carving on the slope gave me to think, but attention has already been focused on this detail in Chapter IV, and a close and prolonged examination of it has convinced me that it was merely a folk-eccentricity of the period. An inability to leave well alone is not infrequently characteristic of amateur performances in the arts and crafts. Either Master Meadows (to accept his existence and responsibility for the moment) was excessively enthusiastic, or he was not much concerned with practical penmanship, or, again, the desk was for reading—not writing. Indeed, all the carving on the desk is in harmony, though the narrow band on the flat top, above the slope, is rather less finished and of a wood now lighter-toned than the rest. This band has been re-set, but is well worn. On the *baron* side (in heraldic parlance) of the slope itself, within one of the largest hearts, are the conjoined intitials C M, G M or D M (the D being reversed and sharing part of the first upright of the M). On the *femme* side, again in large hearts, are the initials S M parted by a small heart superimposed with two arrows in saltire, and, below, the date 1665. The arrowed heart, in its various forms, needs no explanation; and most probably no armorial significance attaches to the *fleurs-de-lys* or the bush of feathers previously mentioned. Anyhow, they have no correspondence to any Meadows or Medows heraldry known to me.

In another respect than those noted in the last paragraph but one, the desk is allied with contemporary ornament, and that is in the presence of a whorl, and a roundel chip-carved with chevron and other decoration. The history of ornament is rich in whorls and roundels which enjoyed a considerable vogue in the thirteenth century. As was also noted in Chapter III, debased attempts to realize a similar effect are sometimes found on boarded chests of late period. Indeed there was in the seventeenth century a marked recrudescence of the taste, perhaps partly encouraged by the rise of the 'Carolean Gothic', and resulting in a minor spate of whorls, geometric roundels and allied ornament, whether on objects professionally made or on those of amateur status.[39]

By way of example, we may note in the former category the under-base rosetting of a standing cup of *lignum vitae* in the Victoria and Albert Museum. English work of mid-seventeenth-century date, this cup ($5\frac{1}{2}$ in. high, 4 in. diam.) was given to the Museum through the National Art-Collections Fund in 1936 in memory of S. Flint Clarkson. Numerous other items could be brought into the reckoning, among them small circular boxes and such things as a pocket-mirror in a chip-carved case which I picked up years ago, at the Caledonian Market for the modest sum of sixpence. Containing its original glass, the case is inlaid on its 'spine' with a crescent between two hearts, and probably belongs to the second half of the seventeenth century. One mentions such things for comparative purposes, though it by no means follows that many of them were anything but town-made. On the other hand, there are objects for which a country origin may well be postulated.

Among items of furniture on which whorls, roundels, or similar ornament appear may be noted the box in Fig. 46, and two others in the Victoria and Albert Museum. Of the two latter boxes, one with its interlaced work (an elaboration of roundelling) is of walnut and is initialled and dated E W 1648. The second and later is of applewood incised T N 1699. Cherubs' heads are among its ornament, which also includes a medallion enclosing a bird on a tree. This box is stated to have come from Exeter.

Of Fig. 46 I know nothing before I bought it of the late Mr J. Rochelle Thomas in King Street, St. James's. Though differently designed, it has some affinity of character with the 1648 box at South Kensington. One is struck by the care with which the design has been set out and carved. Indeed, the best of such work, whether home- or professionally-made, is often very well done according to its standards. In Fig. 46, the lid is covered with stellate roundels; but front and sides have simulated arched compartments enclosing whole and demi-roses and other flowers, counterchanged. There are four hearts. On the back, in a much ruder style, is incised an inaccurate version of the Royal Arms with the lion and unicorn supporters, and the intitials I R. Though corrupt, the achievement may possibly have been adapted from an incised design on a 'poker-work' chest of James I's time, though the box itself belongs to a later period. Whether the arms were *added* to the back of the box (where normally they would be invisible) by an adherent of the exiled second James, opens a problem beyond the scope of the present inquiry. I fancy that I myself originated this rather precarious theory, though some excellent judges have not disagreed with it. In any case, the rendering of the heraldry has somewhat the air of an abandoned trial-piece.

Besides the hearts on it, what fixes this particular box as a 'courting' piece is a posy lightly incised on the front, just under the lid. In a random admixture of upper and lower case lettering, not here reproduced in its full complexity, this jingle reads: 'In stead off Love that I doe o[h?] This Box off Yew I do bestow so be it Alleloi [?]'. The final word is indistinct but may be the letterer's version of 'Alleluia', and 'off Yew' presumably means 'on You', the box being oaken. At the beginning of the verse, but separated from it, are faint marks suggestive of a capital R, possibly a maker's mark.

As said before, such pieces as this are (somewhat superior) expressions of the same folk impulses to which the decorative love-spoons, stay-busks, knitting-sheaths, lace-bobbins and other pieces of equivalent style owe their existence.

Two points must be emphasized here. One is that some of these things might or might not have been love tokens, according to circumstance, and it would be rash to cast our net too widely for 'courting' items. The second point is that the majority of such trifles cannot be assigned to *earlier* than the second half of the eighteenth century when there would seem to have started something of a boom in folk craft, though many of the things made then and later have a strongly traditional character.

That the designs were in fact traditional is shown by such an item as a very interesting love-spoon of Caernarvonshire type in the National Museum of Wales. Actually dated 1667, it is the earliest known to Dr Iorwerth C. Peate, though it exhibits features also found in many examples of much later period. This spoon is inscribed L R and (later) I W. In *The Connoisseur* (January, 1919) W. Ruskin Butterfield illustrated two Knitting-sheaths dated 1684 and 1690. Most knitting-sheaths are of later period than these.

Similar evidence of traditional methods is met with in a combined domino-and-dice box which, with its contents, was given to me, years ago, by my friend Charles R. Beard. This box is made on the 'dug-out' principle (see Chapter III), being hollowed out o the solid wood. Each compartment has a sliding lid, sunk for the reception of since-vanished plaques of another material, such as incised bone or under-painted glass. The sides of the box are chip-carved in traditional style. In default of an authentic date appearing on them, it is often unsafe to assign such items to a narrow period, as they doubtless continued to be made in much the same way for a long while. 'On style,' the projecting thumbpieces of the lids and the general appearance of the box suggest somewhere about the junction of the seventeenth and eighteenth centuries. Let us be on the safe side and call it eighteenth, which is wide enough. I have seen a somewhat similar box, without contents or lid, chip-carved on its carcase with whorls, in the little museum at Sigtuna in Sweden. The folk art of various countries and districts often has much in common; and it is also conceivable that some such boxes were made by mariners to beguile watches below. The fact that in my box the home-made dominoes reach as high as double-nine argues no wish for a quick game: a detail that recommended them to me on certain quiet spells of night duty as an A.R.P. Warden.

Most of those who made such things can never be identified, which is a good reason why the rustic tradition of Susan Meadows' desk should now be put under the critical microscope. This returns us to the late Miss Amelrosa Cobbold of Blythburgh, a daughter of Alan Brooksby Cobbold, and granddaughter of Charles Cobbold[40] by his wife Ann, sole surviving child and heiress of my great-grand-uncle, Owen Roe, of Rose Hill, Ipswich, and Darmsden, near Needham Market, Suffolk. (This 'Ready-Money Roe', as he was known, was uncle to the 'Uncle Owen' whom we met in Chapter I).

It was by this marriage that the Rose Hill and Darmsden properties passed to the Cobbolds; and according to my information it was Mr Alan Brooksby Cobbold who brought away the desk with him on what was probably his one and only visit to 'little Darmsden' at the time of his mother's burial there. That burial was in 1851; and one suspects that it may have been about this time that the desk was repaired, as already noted.

Tradition takes up the tale as follows.[41] The desk was 'carved' by a 'cavalier' named Meadows or Meddow (the spelling is immaterial) who had married Susan, daughter of an earlier Owen Roe, a Puritan. And (added Miss Cobbold) it was due to the Meadows' influence that the Roes were able to 'return' to Darmsden—the inference being that they, as Parliamentarians, had been dispossessed at the Restoration.

Critically handled, the tradition crumbles a little, as might be expected, though not so much as to put it out of court. The 'return' to Darmsden may be discounted as there is no known evidence that the Roes were there at the period. (True, there was a family of Roe of Needham Market nearby, but no connexion has yet been traced between it and the Henley-Westerfield-Darmsden Roes to whom belonged Owen the Puritan.) Again, no evidence emerges to declare the colour of Master Meadows' politics, unless we choose to read an allusion to the Boscobel Oak into the acorn motifs on the desk, and such a reading would need documentary evidence about Master Meadows to support it. Royalists were on the whole scarce in Suffolk at the time of the Civil War, and it is certain that *some* members of the family to which Master Meadows most probably belonged were Parliament men.[42] No less than the infamous iconoclast, Will Dowsing, who in the name of religion wreaked such wanton damage on ancient churches, edges into the picture as a Meadows' relation by marriage. On the other hand, it is clear that later generations of at any rate one branch of the Meadows (Medows) family were so far reconciled as to have place at Court, and to do very well for themselves; and it is a truism that, during the Civil War, the allegiances of families were sharply divided.

But if we cannot decide whether our Master Meadows was Royalist or Parliamentarian, we can reasonably identify Owen Roe the Puritan with an individual who was buried at Dallinghoo on March 12th, 1681-2, and was the direct ancestor of the Darmsden family.[43] Admittedly this Owen is not known to have had a *daughter* named Susan; but he *did* have an *aunt* Susan, who died young and was buried in 1575; and he *did* have a *sister*, Joan, baptized October 5th, 1609, who married one Jeffery *Medowe*, of Newbourn, Suffolk, on October 11th, 1638. Thus, the primary essential of a Meadows—Roe match is established.

I know nothing more of this Jeffery Medowe nor whether he had issue, but Colonel Manvers Meadows, D.S.O., F.S.A., eldest of the Witnesham branch of the family, has kindly informed me that Jeffery certainly came of the stock of which I shall shortly have something to say. We get no forrader by reading the first set of initials on the desk as 'G M' and attempting to expand the G as 'Geoffrey' (for Jeffery) as, apart from anything else, the man of the desk would seem to have belonged to the next generation. If, however, the initials be read as D M conjoined, we have another possibility.

In medieval times and later, there were persons named Meadows (Medowe, Medewe, Medows, etc.) in and around Witnesham, some miles from Newbourn in Suffolk. If we read D M as Daniel Meadows we have a conjunction of names frequently found in the family. Daniel I, of Chattisham Hall which he bought of Sir Robert Hitcham in 1630, will not serve as, for one thing, he died in 1651. Nor can any later Daniel be brought to this judgment, though there were many of them in the family. For example, Colonel Manvers Meadows has pointed out to me that Thomas Meadows (eldest son of Daniel I's brother William of Witnesham Hall) had two sons named Daniel, both of whom are said to have died in infancy, though the fate of one (born in May, 1636) is uncertain. This Thomas 'also owned 200 acres in Darmsden, and must have known Owen Roe, "the Puritan"'. If the initials on the desk are really D M, as I suppose, the possibility of their expansion to Daniel Meadows becomes little short of a certainty.

Other good grounds exist for accepting that the Meadows and Roes were at any rate aware of each other's existence; and on Miss Cobbold's evidence, an old lady named Meadows Taylor, in the nineteenth century, asserted a Meadows—Roe relationship in the terms of the desk's tradition. (According to Brydges' edition of

Collins's *Peerage*, Vol. V (1812), Meadows Taylor, of Diss, attorney, was descended, *ex parte materna*, from old Daniel Meadowe I of Chattisham Hall.) One may therefore be excused for contending that, despite its obvious defects, the tradition of the desk is more than fantasy. Whether the detail that, in 1851, what had been the Roe property at Darmsden was leased by the trustees of Mrs Charles Cobbold to James *Meadows* Moore, of Darmsden, gent.,[44] has a bearing on the desk's later history is beyond me to decide, though the year is the same as that when the desk is said to have been removed from Darmsden by Mr Alan Brooksby Cobbold.

The desk is a piece of home-made type. If we choose to accept the belief that our Master (? Daniel) Meadows carved it for an unrecorded Susan, we may do so without clog of conscience. Indeed we may go further and speculate as to his views on the rise to fortune of a cadet branch of the family to which he may well have belonged. For old Daniel I had a 5th son (Sir) Philip, who relieved Milton as Oliver Cromwell's Latin Secretary, and saw the world in the role of ambassador. He married a Lucy of Charlecote. Their son, Sir Philip II, Knight Marshal of the Palace, married a Boscawen. It was the second Sir Philip's grandson Charles, who discarded his original style in 1788, and assumed the name and arms of Pierrepont, having inherited the estate of his maternal uncle, the 2nd Duke of Kingston, whose luckless match with the notorious Miss Chudleigh resulted in a *cause célèbre*. From being a wealthy commoner, Charles Pierrepont (born Meadows), esquire, rose to the rank of Lord Pierrepont of Holme Pierrepont, Viscount Newark of Newark-on-Trent, and lastly 1st Earl Manvers.

Thus it was that the blood of old Daniel Meadowe I came to course in the veins of a race of Earls—remote kinsmen, be it suggested, of the yeoman-carver of Susan Meadows' Desk. And for me, a student of antique furniture, there remains the singular satisfaction of owning a piece which could so possibly have belonged to a connexion of my forefather who (as we believe) wore buff and iron at Colchester Siege in 1648.

His descendant, my grand-uncle Owen, whose portrait gazes quizzically at me from my Study wall, remembered having seen the Puritan's pistol. It was, he said, a very long one.

12 · Of Pewter Brass, Copper and Iron

FEW things look better in a cottage or country-house than a garnish of pewter to foil the warm and gleaming darks of old oak furniture; but have a care!

Pewter is a ticklish subject, with many pitfalls for those whose enthusiasm for it is unmatched with any but a facile appreciation of its undoubted charm. It so happens that I have honorary membership of a body of learned professors of the study, The Society of Pewter Collectors, but I confess that the more I see of that study the less inclined I am to generalize about it.

If I have said but little about fakes and reproductions in this book, it is because it is often extremely difficult to explain to anyone but a trained observer exactly how one knows a piece to be false, whether it be in woodwork, pottery, metal, or anything else. Successful detection of the false from the true is very much a matter of personal experience, and of seeing and handling as much as one can of both. To any beginner, I would say: study all the examples you know to be modern (*e.g.* obvious fakes and admitted reproductions), and compare their appearance with those that you have good reason to accept as authentic. Quite soon you will begin to differentiate between them on your own account. But never fall into an easy way of thinking that all fakes are obvious. One must treat the faker as one treats an enemy, with a due respect for his powers and resourcefulness. The collector who learns a few 'wrinkles', and imagines he is steeled against every ambush, is asking for trouble. Fortunately many fakers are fools and make bad mistakes, but the shrewdest of them are extremely cunning; and even in the legitimate sphere of honest reproduction things sometimes appear which, perhaps after passing through a few hands and getting a trifle of 'age' on them, may cause a highly experienced student to 'look twice'. One has known of quite good authorities, learned in matters of style and construction or method, and with an excellent basis of documentary reference, who were far less reliable when it came to 'knowing a fake'. But though one should be ever on one's guard, one must avoid that state of mind in which fakes are seen where they do not exist. Not all genuine antiques are dilapidated—even (to return to it) in pewter.

There is good pewter to be had, but also there is a depressing abundance of fakes. So before investing in that baluster-measure, or those pretty little 'nut plates' with their so-convincing touches—have a care! And quite a lot of the candlesticks are early nineteenth-century at best—and not 'Queen Anne' as you may have fondly believed. Indeed, much of the old pewter awaiting the 'small collector' and suitable for cottage homes is of late period, though some of it is pleasant enough. Experienced buyers are mainly interested in earlier stuff—still obtainable from certain reputable dealers, among other sources; but the average tankard, small measure, pepper-pot, trencher-salt or what-have-you is of late eighteenth- or early nineteenth-century date. Don't forget, too, that the glass-bottomed tankard is a modern variety. While contemplating the theme of this book, I noticed, in an obscure corner of a village shop, the broken-off base of a pewter candlestick of a type of the second half of the seventeenth century. Curiosity impelled me to handle the piece. The breakage was the only convincing thing about it.

Candlesticks! They light us straight into the twinkling land of polished brass, so much appreciated and (on average) so little understood: territory in which candlesticks of any period are a-jumbled with Horse Brasses about which such a deal has been written. Admittedly, they have a fascination, these Horse Brasses, but they were not made (except in modern times) for indoor ornament, and the great majority of them are of no great age. There would be much difficulty in tracing any reliable continuity between the small pendant plaques, frequently enamelled with armorial and other devices, used in some cases as harness ornaments in medieval times, and the later English Horse Brasses. Of the latter, by far the most are at oldest Victorian, though some are earlier, and one has but the slightest expectation of picking up anything pre-dating the eighteenth century. Personally, I have yet to handle a seventeenth-century English Horse Brass.

This scarcity discourages one's faith in romantic derivations of this or that form of ornament from types 'brought home by crusaders', or from motifs favoured by the priesthood of Astarte. For what it is worth, my impression is that a truer analogy between the average English Horse Brass and a remote antiquity is more likely to have been by way of the ornamental braces or suspenders as worn by the hardy men of Switzerland and the Tyrol. There is no reason why we should not enjoy and study the Horse Brass, but we can at least spare ourselves the folly of being unduly fanciful about it.

Brass candlesticks, as those in other materials including pewter, have, however, a true continuity in England from early times. The slender, slightly knopped sticks of the fifteenth and early sixteenth centuries are now so scarce as to be all but unprocurable, and the mid-seventeenth-century type, with drip-pan midway up the shaft, has become 'very desirable'. In itself, the spasmodic rise of the drip-pan from the spreading base to the nozzle of the candlestick is a fascinating study. It was not a consistent development, for in the late seventeenth and earlier part of the eighteenth century the old drip-pan-*cum*-base was very prevalent, and it is not until approximately the middle of the eighteenth century that the nozzle-drip-pan became firmly and more or less continuously established. To differentiate between the various types of eighteenth-century candlestick is impossible in the space at command, but the collector will do well to familiarize himself with the elegance of, say, the earlier types, and to distinguish between them and the clumsy baluster forms of the late eighteenth-early nineteenth century—so different from the balusters of the second half of the seventeenth (Figs. 54 & 55). Of the ancient form of stick known as the 'pricket'—from its spike on which to impale the candle—nothing much need be said as later examples in brass are mainly continental and intended for ecclesiastical use.

Of other forms of illuminant mostly in iron, the lantern, 'rush-jack,' and the hanging lamp known in North Britain as the 'crusie' should at least be mentioned. Lanterns were used medievally, but most of the obtainable examples of antique lantern are much later in date. One small type made decorative, in brass, is represented by that attributed to Charles II's rescuer Jane Lane, as illustrated in Allan Fea's *After Worcester Fight* (1904; f.p.42). I have recently handled a lantern of what seemed to be a somewhat similar type, but was tempted to assign this second example to a later period than that of the worthy Mistress Jane—Lady Fisher, to give her her married name.

Rush-light holders of iron must have been of frequent occurrence in country-homes. Most examples date from the seventeenth or eighteenth centuries, a usual form being that in which the iron stick is fixed in a wooden base. Rather more rarely, stick and base are all of iron. Of such, an interesting type is that in which the twisted iron base is formed like an inverted 'cup', closely similar to the open-work 'cup' finials surmounting a well-known type of seventeenth-century firedog (Figs. 52 & 53). Such 'rush-jacks' as this are very scarce. I own a couple: one—a beauty—bought by my father in London; the other found by Charles R. Beard in Ireland.

Medieval Firedogs or Andirons are the province of the elect, but examples from the seventeenth century onwards are obtainable. Fuller's *Worthies* (1662) differentiates between the terms, declaring that the dogs bore the 'burthen of the fuel', whereas the 'brazen-andirons stand only for state', but there are sundry instances in which the function was obviously dual. Small dogs, to bear the wood, were sometimes known as 'creepers,' and andirons supplied with hooks to carry the spits were at any rate sometimes known as 'cob-irons' or 'copirons', though the term 'spit-dogs' is also used. A very prevalent type of dog is that with a short upright scrolled over at the top, these mostly belonging to the eighteenth century.

A lingering trace of the firedog is found in the fire-iron supports forming a part of many old-fashioned Fenders. For practical purposes, the history of the unattached Fender begins in the second half of the seventeenth century,[45] and it is tempting to conjecture that the devastation caused by the Great Fire of London in 1666 was not without its effect in popularizing this article of hearth-furniture. Most examples are, however, of considerably later date. Here should also be mentioned that useful device the wire Fender or Fire-Guard, which has been rather rashly claimed as an American invention, as it was certainly known in England in the eighteenth century. Such pieces have continued to be made in more or less traditional forms right down to modern times.

Of Fire-Backs, so often made, like many Fire-dogs, of Sussex iron, little need be said, though the beginner should take note that many old types have been reproduced commercially. A good English fire-back of any antiquity can be pleasant, useful and interesting. Once when my father happened to be visiting Westerham, in Kent, he noticed one, dated 1772, doing duty as the doorstep of a cottage close to Wolfe's birthplace, had the ponderous mass of metal turned up with a spade, and bought it for the proverbial song. Much earlier—and finer—backs have been found in no less easy circumstances, but those happy-hunting days are one with the ages.

Of Fire-Irons, I propose to mention one class only, the Ember or

Brand-Tongs, pleasant things such as can be seen in action in Seymour Lucas' well-known picture of *The Smoker*: a cavalier lighting his clay with a glowing ember picked from the fire. Such seventeenth- and eighteenth-century tongs frequently possess tobacco-stopper attachments. I have a good pair of these tongs, with both its pivot-pin and the end of one handle fashioned as stoppers (Fig. 53). It is of eighteenth-century date, and a practical test has shown that the stoppers are too bulky for use on 'clays' of earlier period. This particular pair is known to have come from Lingfield Place, Surrey. But to discuss all the various forms of hearth-furniture in general, including such things as Pork- or Toasting-Forks, Toasters, Chestnut Roasters, and Mullers or Ale-Warmers of the funnel or 'shoe' forms (Fig. 52), would be unduly to extend the scope of this book. I have a brass shoe-type Muller of early nineteenth-century date, engraved with an esquire's helmet between the initials D H. Whether the helmet (which is not mounted on a torse or heraldic wreath) was the owner's badge, or merely advertised to all and sundry that D H was a gent., or what, I have not fathomed.

On the other hand, a word may be spared for the Door Porter or Door Stop, usually of brass or iron when it is not of glass, as these things, though of late occurrence, are interesting and decidedly useful in the home. Of the glass Porters, resembling large and heavy paper weights, of greenish bubbly metal frequently enclosing floral motifs, and made at such places as Bristol, Stourbridge, Wakefield, Castleford, etc., it is only necessary to add that some are as old as the late eighteenth-early nineteenth century, though many are later and modern 'revivals' are numerous. Porters of brass or iron were much favoured in the first half of the nineteenth century, though some types are obviously later. Those with figure motifs, such as (appropriately) the 'Iron Duke', Punch and Judy, or Ally Sloper (the last of late nineteenth-century origin) can often be dated with precision. For example, the seated Punch cannot be earlier than 1849 as it is borrowed from the still familiar *Punch* cover by 'Dicky' Doyle, whose design was first used in that year. Metal porters were made at many places, including Coalbrookdale and Lambeth, and some of them are noticeably related to those cast-iron Chimneypiece Ornaments, of which the Lion and the Stooked Wheatsheaf are especially common.

Finally, and not to exhaust the reader's patience, there are candle-snuffers (usually eighteenth- or nineteenth-century, though much older examples rarely occur) and such survivals as the Bed-Wagon and the Warming-Pan, both of which served a similar purpose to the modern hot-water bottle. Of these, the Warming-Pan—'a harmless, a useful, and I will add, gentlemen, a comforting article of domestic furniture'—is much the more decorative, and it is to be supposed that decoration is now its main purpose in the home. Antique examples are usually of eighteenth- or early nineteenth-century date—those with plain, tubular, iron handles are certainly late—but the idea is considerably older than this. Any chance to acquire an example of pre-eighteenth century date should not be neglected.

Serjeant Buzfuz's celebrated allusion to the Warming-Pan has already been quoted; but if we do not need reminding of the 'Warming-Pan Plot' (1688), we should not forget the examinee who so narrowly escaped its correct definition: 'The Pretender was so-called because it was pretended that he was born in a warming-pan.'[46] For that is as admirable as, in its way, is the doubtless truer story about Dr Dee's disreputable associate, Edward Kelley, who claimed to have transmuted a piece of a warming-pan into gold. At any rate, he sent to Queen Elizabeth a warming-pan with a hole cut in it, and piece of gold which fitted the hole! It was all very interesting. But as this is a country book, it is more appropriate to recall one of Arthur Morrison's short stories based on the character of 'Cunning Murrell', a local wise man and horse-leech, who actually lived at Hadleigh in Essex, where he died in 1856. In this attractive tale, two bibulous souls referred the disputed ownership of a jar of liquor (which belonged to neither party) to Cunning Murrell's magic mirror, which never responded to anyone telling an untruth. After each man had given a highly imaginative account of what he had seen in the mirror, the sage shrewdly remarked that both must be lying as he had not shown them the mirror at all, but merely the lid of an old warming-pan. And it was Murrell who kept the jar of liquor!

This may be fiction, but it well illustrates the essential shrewdness of the old country life.

13 · Of Storied Furniture

GIVEN the financial means to do so, anybody can form a magnificent collection on the trained advice of others, but such is not collecting as understood by the elect. To the latter, collecting is an extremely personal affair: a matter both serious and romantically exciting. Admittedly, few nowadays will plead guilty to a romantic urge. It is a suspect term implying a measure of irresponsibility and a lack of scientific detachment; but, for all that, I have yet to meet a blown-in-the-glass collector who was any the worse for a touch of it. For one thing, it implies imagination, and though, in studies, imagination must be ridden on the curb, a properly controlled use of it sometimes yields extremely valuable results. Your student who clings tamely to the facts without attempting any deductions from them may do some excellent spade-work, but, so far as any creative aspect of his craft is concerned, he stays in the respectable 'navvy' class.

In thus defending (as I stoutly do) the more imaginative aspect of collecting, I am very far from countenancing those unreasoned flights of fancy that will always be the bugbear of seriously intentioned students. Among the most rampant forms of it are the fantastic stories which have somehow or other attached themselves not only to blatant forgeries, but to respectable antiquities. I remember, many years ago, being solemnly assured that a much carved, but doubtless genuine, boarded chest was in some way associated with Margaret of Anjou, consort of the saintly Henry VI. Why? Because its overloaded surface-ornament included certain formal flowers believed to represent *marguerites*, and Margaret of Anjou is known to have used the badge of a *daisy*, punning on her name. The detail that Margaret died in 1482 and that this chest (as I remember it) was at the earliest of sixteenth-century fashion had not interfered with an otherwise pleasing theory.

Still more romantic in association are the divers chests linked with the story of the 'Mistletoe Bough': the affianced damsel who hid herself in a chest in a game of hide-and-seek, and was not discovered until she had choked her life out in its fusty grip. That such tragedies have happened does not make it any the easier to pin down to a particular piece of furniture the tale of 'young Lovel's' skeleton bride.

Frankly, I do not know how many chests have been accredited as the true 'original' of that in the 'Mistletoe Bough', though I have certainly heard of one, and seem to have heard of others. Since it is not my wish to wound anyone's pride of ownership, I am willing to concede that one of these chests is the actual piece referred to in the Gothick carol—not perhaps that it gets us much forrader. And that, in a book devoted to country furniture, is about as far as I am ready to commit myself.

On the other hand, I remember hearing of one chest with a bony association that was quite probably a country piece, and this demands our closer attention. In 1922, a section of the Press excited its readers with accounts of a grisly find at a London antique dealer's.

Among some furniture obtained in the course of business by a firm at Shepherd's Bush was a framed chest, its panels carved with a simple form of simulated arcading. From illustrations in the *Evening News* of January 31st, 1922, and the *Daily Mail* of February 1st, 1922, I do not doubt that this somewhat battered relic was a genuine seventeenth-century piece, and that, as then stated, it had possibly come 'from somewhere in the country'.

Now, within this chest were certain bones which 'when pieced together made the skeleton of an adult person'. The chest with its contents was dumped on the pavement outside the shop. A woman passer-by stopped, lifted the lid—and fainted.

In due course, the chest (complete with bones) went to a West End dealer, where further notice was taken of it. As the skeleton was said to be female, and women are news, the story got into the newspapers.

I do not know what was the result of the ensuing inquest, if such were held, but from the published accounts of the matter in my possession it at least seems possible that here was one of those instances of an anatomical specimen being dumped in a handy receptacle where it lay forgotten. As was reasonably argued in the *Daily Mail* at the time, it would have been 'impossible for anyone getting inside [the chest] . . . to have starved to death without having made her voice heard some considerable distance'.

All of which reminds me of a story my father used to tell [47] and which I now take leave to re-tell as best I can. True or otherwise, it is of a sort which might have happened, and if its humour is grimly Rowlandsonian it is not without its value as a comment on bygone manners. So, then, to our tale . . .

One wild and wintry night, a belated traveller sought shelter at a lonely farmhouse in a remote country district. He did not feel too happy about it; there was a sinister something about the place; but he was lost and there was nowhere else for him to lay his head.

Shown into a bedroom, he made fast the door as well as he could, and then took stock of his surroundings. It was one of those occasions when every horrid tale one has ever heard springs forcibly to mind. To make reasonably sure of safety, the traveller raised the lid of a chest which stood in the room—and saw lying within it the unmistakable corpse of an old man.

Dropping the lid, the traveller glanced fearfully about him. Nothing moved but the flickering shadows cast by the candle-light. One gathers that his night was not particularly peaceful.

On rising, the haggard traveller melodramatically faced his down-looking hosts with dark hints. Their secret, he said, was known.

They, puzzled by the strange behaviour of an obvious 'furriner', asked him what all the fuss was about? 'Oh,' said they, when enlightened, 'that's only granfeyther. He passed away natural, so we salted un down till the frost breaks!'

Any countryman will appreciate the force of that story; but from considering one of the less orthodox uses of the chest, we may advantageously pass to another of less macabre import. In the *Morning Post* of November 12th, 1929, appeared a news-item which demands a place in this rambling record.

'Relics of the day when farmers had to pay tithe in kind, some old corn chests which had not seen the light for 200 years have been unearthed at Middleton-in-Teesdale Rectory.

'In one of them was a quantity of corn evidently part of the tithe. It is to be sown in the parish.'

Thus ran the report and, though I have not tested it, it arouses profitable speculation.

As an example of true, as opposed to false, historical reconstruction, an oak desk inherited by Mr Charles Partridge, M.A., F.S.A., affords a good example of documentation. Dating from *circa* 1650, this interesting piece is fitted with a number of drawers inside, and on the sinister side of the exterior with a long drawer which can be secured by a bolt from within. In all probability, the desk belonged to Mr Partridge's ancestor, Robert Partridge of Holton St Mary, Suffolk, yeoman, who in his will (7th December 1675) left to his son, Robert, his 'Deske in my Chamber called the best Chamber.' Earlier, a list of household goods (1667) belonging to Partridge's neighbour Daniel Wall, of Stratford St Mary, Suffolk, mentions a 'deskbox', and it may be that Partridge bought the piece at the sale of Wall's effects.[48] For continuity of possession in a family of good yeomen origin, this desk even surpasses the more complicated descent of 'Susan Meadows' Desk', as set forth elsewhere in this book.

It should be now obvious that the purpose of this chapter is not merely to assemble a collection of entertaining anecdotes, but to aid beginners in distinguishing between the various sorts of 'history' that may be dished up for their delectation. In other words, the anecdotes are chosen with intent. Careful scrutiny of these various stories will show that they range from the obviously impossible to the superficially credible, and from the circumstantial to the study with a solid basis of documentation. At this stage, one may usefully revive a problem partaking in some degree of all four categories, though in what proportions it is less easy to decide.

On the night before he fell to the conquering Tudor at Bosworth Field in the August of 1485, King Richard III of bloody memory is stated to have lain—not in his ghost-ridden tent, as Shakespeare has it—but on his military bed, at a house which later became the *Blue Boar* at Leicester. This bed was his own property, his *lit-à-camp*, brought with him, and not a chattel of his temporary lodging. At the *Blue Boar* there was later shown a large posted bedstead, widely famed as King Richard's. The story goes that, in the latter part of the sixteenth century, a 'jumbling' of this bedstead accidentally disclosed a hoard of gold coins in its double-bottom. At the beginning of James I's reign, the goodwife who had made the discovery was foully murdered, thus helpfully augmenting the growing crop of tradition. Later still, the bedstead more than once changed owners, suffering the loss of its feet in the process.[49]

Now, the tradition of the bedstead having been King Richard's was no mushroom growth. As Beard has pointed out, it was known early in the seventeenth century and 'must have been established long before'.[50] Antiquaries have their own good reasons for not swallowing such yarns without mastication, and in this case two bulky objections stuck in the gullets of many. Military commanders are not wont to encumber themselves on campaign with large and heavy bedsteads; and even had Richard done so, he would not have chosen a piece of the Elizabethan period, for such the bed in question was deemed to be. Wherefore, it seemed feasible that though this bedstead might have been truly linked with the story of the treasure-finding, that part of the tale attributing it to the last 'Plantagenet' ruler of England was a picturesque accretion. In this, critics found support in the numerous cases of antiquities somehow or other acquiring a mythic history by intent or confusion on the part of the tellers.

So far, so good; but the fact remains that a Leicester historian named James Thompson (1817-1877) proffered a theory which, so far as I know, has not been fully investigated. Thompson announced as his opinion—I again quote Beard[50]—that 'though the bed as then existing was undoubtedly of late sixteenth-century fashion, all the features that gave it this late character—the posts and tester—were impositions upon a simple panelled bed-stock of a much earlier date, which he saw no reason to believe was other than of the latter part of the fifteenth century.' If this were so, the possibility of the actual bedstead, as apart from its later 'trimmings', having been used by King Richard would at once be reinstated.

Here I must needs call a halt to the matter, merely adding that though such an act as the sixteenth-century embellishment of a fifteenth-century piece is unusual, it is not impossible, if merely on the grounds that a limited amount of antique furniture gives clear evidence of incorporating re-used material. At the same time, this is, on the face of it, one of the many cases of picturesquely-pedigreed furniture that should be approached with circumspection. Unfortunately, I have not seen the bedstead myself and know no more than did my friend Beard whether the problem has since been satisfactorily solved one way or t'other, but it seems certain that the bedstead's most spectacular features are no earlier than the reign of Elizabeth.

It may here be recalled that in 1909 a carved oak armchair was noticed in the press as having been that used by Richard III's opponent, Henry Tudor, Earl of Richmond, so soon to become King Henry VII. The occasion was supposed to have been a council of war held before Bosworth Field at the old *Three Tuns* at Atherstone. The suggestion was made that King Edward VII might use this, his royal ancestor's seat, at a levee, but as it transpired that the chair was of considerably later period than that claimed for it, the proposal fell through. Judged from a newspaper illustration,[51] the chair, though doubtless antique, was altogether more consistent with the first half of the seventeenth century than with the latter part of the fifteenth. Beyond doubt, the tradition of its use by the Tudor was advanced in all innocence and sincerity, but it would seem that the antiquarian facts were rightly invoked against it.

Mention of Shakespeare's *Tragedy of King Richard III* reminds one that many fantastical tales have been told of furniture attributed to the possession of our greatest dramatist, but on these it were better to touch in a clean last chapter.

14 · Of Shakespeare and certain Trees

LET me say here and now that this book is in no wise concerned with problems centred in the authorship of Shakespeare's plays. For my part, I am a convinced though (I hope) reasonable Stratfordian, and shall hold to that way unless other than special pleading and an ingenious manipulation of facts be adduced to change my opinion. For present purposes, I am solely concerned with William Shakespeare as the countryman he undoubtedly was, and the detail that a mass of rubbish has been written about 'his' furniture has no bearing either way on his responsibility as a playwright and poet.

It is quite clear that none of the furniture associated with Shakespeare's name can be proved to have been in his ownership: a fact by no means surprising when we reflect how relatively seldom *any* antique furniture can be definitely assigned to its original possessors. All the same, certain 'Shakespearean' pieces were existent in his time, including (in the Birthplace) the Grammar School Desk already referred to, the carved oak armchair from the *Falcon* at Bidford, and (in the Shakespeare Memorial) a chair-table doubtfully said to have come from the poet's brother Gilbert. Of these three pieces, the desk may very well have been seen and even used by the youthful bard; the Bidford chair, though contemporary with him, has no reliable pedigree; and the chair-table came from an obscure family of Shakespeares at Wootton Wawen who, just possibly, may have enjoyed a remote kinship with the poet. In *The Connoisseur* (July, 1940) my father and I discussed this interesting item in all the detail we could discover, showing that although the chair-table had lost its movable back, the lack of which had been compensated by the intrusion of part of a leathered chair of 'Cromwellian' type, the main structure in all probability existed in William Shakespeare's lifetime.

The like may be said of the celebrated 'courting settle' in the living-room at the Hathaway Cottage at Shottery. To suggest that Shakespeare found it convenient to follow a not unusual custom of lovemaking on a settle may not be susceptible of proof, but that the settle in point was known to him is probable. It exhibits mouldings of at the least seventeenth-century date, and, in my father's opinion, is old enough for Shakespeare to have seen the piece in place. In other words, a statement that 'the furniture was not in the cottage in Shakespeare's time' needs modification.

So, too, in the case of the famous posted bedstead with caryatids on its back, in an upstairs room at the Shottery Cottage. That this bedstead actually *belonged* to Anne Hathaway herself, rather than to the head of the Hathaway family, may be doubted. But that Anne Hathaway (Shakespeare) may have used it is quite probable. The bedstead is of appropriate quality and period: just such a piece as one might expect to find in a yeoman home of the requisite calibre. Admittedly, there is no evidence that it was not bought, second-hand, and brought to the house at a later date: but there is also no evidence to show that it was. Clearly this is a piece that must have been brought to the house in parts, and assembled within it. And it is not the sort of thing that, once assembled, would be easily removed. In modern times, this excellent item of Elizabethan furniture has been tightened up, so that its posts no longer lean at the picturesque angles familiar to us in many old views of it; but its genuineness and condition are irreproachable. In any antiquarian sense, it is one of the most desirable beds in the world, and that William Shakespeare and his Anne knew it well is a dream that need fear no rude awakening.

Another piece of furniture which must have been known to the poet and his father is the interesting drawered press belonging to the Corporation of Stratford-upon-Avon. This 'new cubborde of boxes' was made in 1595 by one, Lawrence Abelle, in sixteen and a half days. The year is interesting to us, as it was in 1596 that the poet's son Hamnet was buried; in 1596 that the first draft of a grant of the now celebrated Shakespeare coat-armour was committed to paper; and in 1597 that the poet purchased New Place where, according to a respectable tradition, he later planted the famous mulberry tree.

Of the numerous articles made, or reputedly made, notably by Thomas Sharp, from that mulberry tree after its felling in 1756, this is scarcely the place to treat in detail. A similar reservation applies to items carved from the timber of the original Boscobel Oak, the wreck of the *Royal George*, or the various other trees or woods which have captured the fancy of the romantically minded.[52] Such 'relics' cover a wide range from pipe-stoppers to caskets and goblets, and even to an occasional larger item of furniture. (I am here thinking more particularly of the mulberry tree, as there is, in Nash's House at Stratford-upon-Avon, a circular table, made in 1825, its top veneered with wood secured by William Hunt when the tree was felled.) In all the more popular instances, it doubtless happened that the true and original supply of material was in time supplemented from other sources, though in an affidavit dated 14th October 1799, now in Nash's House, Stratford-upon-Avon, Thomas Sharp repudiated having ever 'worked. Sold or Substituted any other Wood than what came from & was part of the said Tree'. It is, however, wise to examine the pedigree of any such relics for, at any rate by some persons, the supply was obligingly suited to meet the demand. In such commercially profitable enthusiasms one may trace an analogous urge to that which provided a steady stream of saintly relics in the medieval past. It was, in short, the old relic-urge dereligionized. I am not suggesting that the early and best authenticated relics of the mulberry tree, the Boscobel Oak, and so forth are lacking in interest. Some, indeed, are historic; but they virtually constitute a separate department of study—a study demanding a cool head and a circumspect approach.

Such coolness would have saved the propagation of a deal of nonsense about divers pieces of household furniture reputedly, but more than dubiously, owned by the poet himself. One of these must serve as an example of the sort of thing I have in mind.

In 1903, a corner-cupboard came under notice. As the story goes, it was found in an extremely dirty state by a farmer at Driffield in Yorkshire. Cleaning it, he found it to be carved with various matters including 'battle axes and other old-time implements', and, better still, 'William Shakespeare' and '1603'. When the theory was advanced that the carving was 'probably' by Shakespeare himself, the prospect became even rosier.

At this point we may turn to an account of the corner-cupboard in question as published in *The Ancestor* (Constable & Co., Ltd.; July, 1903, p.151). According to the writer of the note (whom one suspects from his style to have been none other than the erudite Oswald Barron), the cupboard presented certain peculiarities. 'The curious will only remark of it that the bard, solacing his Stratford hours with the pleasant art of wood-carving, chose for his subject a corner cupboard of a type familiar enough in the early eighteenth century. He was however not for an age but for all time. . . .'

Nor was this all. The name on the cupboard was 'carved not in bold capitals, as is the wont of names upon ancient furniture, but in a handwriting which strengthens the authenticity of the already known signatures of Shakespeare. . . . Many who are unfamiliar with letters of Elizabethan script have professed themselves unable to decipher letter by letter the Shakespearian signatures. The name upon the door shows Shakespeare himself in the same difficulty. Forced by his task to carve letters of greater distinctness than paper or parchment demands, Master William Shakespeare exhibits a lamentable inability to understand or to form the written letters of his period.'

Let us turn for contrast to the Long Table illustrated in Fig. 24, a substantial piece of 'yeoman' status. Now this is unquestionably genuine, and what is more it was found in a farmhouse near Stratford-upon-Avon. Writing of it in *The Connoisseur* (December, 1920), my father inclined to the view that it 'may have been *in situ* when the greatest of dramatists returned to his native town to spend his remaining days at "New Place"—it was almost certainly there when the Irelands made their Warwickshire pilgrimage in 1794, and the frontless William Henry of that name projected his astonishing series of Shakespeare forgeries. It has figured, since its purchase, in several well-known pictures, among them being Mr J. Seymour Lucas's *A 'Whip' for Van Tromp* (R.A., 1883)'. From Lucas, it passed to my maternal Grandfather, Sydney Williams Lee. Time and again, have I sat at it.

Such tables are now all but to seek, and justifiably command prices immensely greater than what was paid for this highly desirable country piece when it was found. Did I mention that price? It was £5! Were I 'after' such a treasure to-day, I might expect to be quoted in hundreds for it by anyone who knew.

Come to think of it, there is romance and to spare in that one scrap of history!

Notes

[1] Thomas Henry Huxley: *Lectures and Essays* (Thinker's Library ed., 1931), p. vii.

[2] C. Reginald Grundy: *A Catalogue of the Pictures and Drawings in the Collection of Frederick John Nettlefold*. Vol. III (1937), pp. 94-95.

[3] Fred Roe, R.I.: *Old Oak Furniture* (1905; 2nd ed. 1908), p. 4. The piece in question is illustrated in the frontispiece to *Old Oak Furniture*. It later entered the collection of our old friend, the late Major-General Sir Coleridge Grove, K.C.B.

[4] Will of Christopher Roe, of Debach, co. Suffolk. P.P.R., Somerset House, Ruthen, fo. 96, 1657-60.

[5] Bar-counters are a relatively modern feature of public houses. George Cruikshank shows one in his plate of *The Gin Shop* in *Sketches by Boz* (1836). Without having studied their history, I should scarcely expect to find them at a much earlier date than that.

[6] H. Clifford Smith, M.A., F.S.A.: *Victoria and Albert Museum: Catalogue of English Furniture and Woodwork*, Vol. II (1930), pp. 19-20.

[7] In architecture, coffering consists of 'sunk panels, caissons or lacunaria formed in ceilings, vaults, and domes'. (I quote from Sir Banister Fletcher's ever-useful *History of Architecture*).

[8] *vide* Fred Roe, R.I.: *Ancient Coffers and Cupboards* (1902) pl. facing p. 43.

[9] 'By architectural writers such figures are called Caryatids, on account of a statement of Vitruvius (i., chap. 1) that women of Carya (more correctly Caryae), a town of Arcadia, were represented as architectural supports—a punishment which, so at least we are told, they incurred for betraying the Greeks to the Persians.' (Arthur H. Smith: *A Guide to the Department of Greek and Roman Antiquities in the British Museum*, 4th ed., 1912, p. 54).

[10] I owe the details to a note taken by my father at the time when we saw this chest-front together.

[11] Chancery Proceedings, Ser. II, Bdl. 156, No. 47. I owe an abstract of the suit to Mr Richard Holworthy. Anthony Rooe was buried at Debach on 4th Dec., 1584; I have not encountered any evidence to suggest that he recovered the Melton property.

[12] R. W. Symonds: *The Chest and the Coffer*, in *The Connoisseur*, January, 1941.

[13] John William Burgon: *The Life and Times of Sir Thomas Gresham* (1839). Vol. I, pp. 403-404.

[14] Burgon: *op cit.*, Vol. I, p. 244 (Clough was factor at Antwerp for Sir Thomas Gresham, Founder of the Royal Exchange, London).

[15] Pedigree compiled by Richard Heape, and included in *The Records of the Family of Heape* of which he was joint author. According to this Dionis (Dennis) Grundie's will was dated 25th February, 1633-34, and proved at Chester 1637. I am of opinion that this Dennis Grundie was not improbably ancestor of the late C. Reginald Grundy, sometime Editor of *The Connoisseur*.

[16] Oswald Barron, F.S.A.: *The Delafields and the Empire*, in *The Ancestor*, No. XI, October, 1904, pp. 119-120.

[17] See F. Gordon Roe: *In the Likeness of Books*, in *Antiques* (New York), February, 1940, where the objects described are illustrated.

[18] There was admittedly a longish interval between the respective 'discoveries'.

[19] It seems necessary nowadays to explain this term 'kernoozing', related to the old Kernoozers' Club, itself an anglicism for 'connoisseurs'.

Notes

[20] In *Old Oak Furniture* (1905), my father described this chair as having remained 'in a neglected state in a barn adjacent to a ruined priory', and as having been 'sold with some other effects during the distress occasioned by a series of bad years, culminating in the disastrous summer of 1903'. I am not clear as to the significance of this passage. My impression is that the chair was brought to Aylesbury from one of the outlying villages. On the other hand, Aylesbury itself once had a house of Grey Friars, long destroyed, and a part of the town is still known as the 'Friarage'. The chair subsequently passed into the collection of the late S. Morgan Williams, of St Donat's Castle, Glamorganshire, and figured in his sale at Christie's on April 26th, 1921.

[21] Information from the late Canon Charles Kirkby Robinson, D.D., Master of St Catherine's College, Cambridge, who gave the chair to my father in 1903. Canon Robinson died in 1909 at his country residence, Risplith, near Ripon, Yorks, aged 83.

[22] For a fuller discussion of 'Mortuary Chairs' and their tradition, see F. Gordon Roe: *Charles I's Head?* in *The Connoisseur*, December, 1945.

[23] R. W. Symonds: *The Windsor Chair*, in *Apollo*, August, 1935. In this article (p. 67) Mr Symonds observed that 'apparently its [the Windsor chair's] manufacture was originally confined to London and its environs, and to Berkshire and Buckinghamshire, especially the last named, owing to the abundance of beech trees'. He also points out that 'Wycombe chair' was, at any rate at one time, an alternative name (p. 69).

[24] Thomas Hamilton Ormsbee: *The Story of American Furniture* (1946), p. 193.]

[25] R. W. Symonds: *The Windsor Chair, II*, in *Apollo*, November, 1935, p. 266. [I am reminded of how in their boyhood my father and his two brothers used a special name for certain chairs in their Cambridge home. They called them 'dairns'. I have always accepted this as an instance of 'private language', such as occurs in some families; but is it possible that 'dairn' was an unconscious orchestration of 'Dan' (Dan Day) ?]

[26] H. Clifford Smith, M.A., F.S.A.: *Victoria and Albert Museum—Catalogue of English Furniture and Woodwork*, Vol. II (1930), p. 4.

[27] On this, see Charles H. Hayward: *English Period Furniture* (1936), p. 22.

[28] I. Herbert: *Roberte the Devyll. A Metrical Romance from an Ancient Illuminated Manuscript* (London; 1798).

[29] Burgon: *op. cit.*, Vol. II, p. 402. (Frances, Duchess of Suffolk, was a niece of the blood of Henry VIII, and mother, also, of the ill-starred 'Jane the quene' (Lady Jane Grey).

[30] G. K. Chesterton: *St Francis of Assisi* (1923), p. 9.

[31] R. W. Symonds: *The Evolution of the Cupboard*, in *The Connoisseur*, December, 1943; also *The Dyning Parlor and its Furniture*, *op. cit.*, January, 1944.

[32] J. R. Fawcett Thompson: *Ioan Daniel's Deu-darn*, in *The Connoisseur*, February, 1928, pp. 100-101.

[33] Fred Roe, R.I., *ibid.*, p. 101.

[34] Fred Roe, R.I.: *Essex Bygones, Pt. II.*, in *The Connoisseur*, January, 1920, p. 26. An illustration of the piece is on p. 27.

[35] Charles R. Beard: *The Romance of Treasure Trove* (1933), p. 278.

[36] On Mistress Penn and the Spinning-Wheel, see Ernest Law: *The History of Hampton Court Palace in Tudor Times* (1885); F. Gordon Roe: *Portrait of a Ghost*, in *The Connoisseur*, December, 1943; and Philip Lindsay: *Hampton Court, A History* (1948).

[37] The substance of this chapter, here considerably extended with additional matter, appeared in *The Connoisseur*, September, 1946, from which it is reproduced by kind permission of the Editor.

[38] Similar customs in Scandinavia and Switzerland are noted by Dr. Iorwerth C. Peate. On Welsh Love-Spoons, see also Owen Evan-Thomas: *Domestic Articles of Wood* (1932). For the old English and Continental custom of giving a 'pair of knives' to a bride, see Charles R. Beard: *Wedding Knives*, in *The Connoisseur*, February, 1930.

[39] The strongly traditional character of the ornament on certain fonts erected after the Restoration is in line with this tendency. (*E.g.* the roundels on the font dated 1662 at Wirksworth, Derbyshire; *repr.* Cox and Harvey: *English Church Furniture* (1907), p. 176.)

[40] Charles Cobbold (1793-1859) was a son of John Cobbold (1746-1835), of The

Notes

Cliff, Ipswich, by his second wife, Elizabeth, daughter of Robert Knipe, of Liverpool, and widow of William Clarke, of Ipswich. She, the 'Ipswich Poetess', figures in the Suffolk classic, *Margaret Catchpole*, written by another of her sons, the Rev. Richard Cobbold (1797-1877). She is thought by some to have been the 'original' of 'Mrs Leo Hunter' in *Pickwick*, though there are other claimants to that distinction.

41 Material collated from letters in the Author's possession from J. Seymour Lucas, R.A., to Fred Roe, R.I., 20th May, 1916, and from Miss Amelrosa Cobbold, to the Author, 29th January, and 15th March, 1924. Mr Lucas gave the name as 'Meddow', which approximates to the more ancient spellings. With certain necessary exceptions, the form 'Meadows' is preferred in this book.

42 An assertion that the Royalist Sir Thomas Medowe, of Great Yarmouth, sprang from the later Witnesham—Coddenham Meadows is groundless (*vide* Rev. Wm. C. Pearson in *The East Anglian: Notes and Queries*, N.S., Vol. V, p. 22).

43 See F. Gordon Roe: *Austerity in Art*, in *The Connoisseur*, March, 1943; also *Notes and Queries*, 1922.

44 Counterpart Lease, 1st November, 1851 in Cobbold archives. Mrs Charles Cobbold died 29th November, 1851.

45 That is in England. The Victoria and Albert Museum has an Italian fender of the sixteenth century. Of iron, it is independent and fashioned as a series of curves. A very interesting example of a wrought steel fender of foliated scroll design was discovered by Messrs Pratt & Son, of London, in an extremely rusty state. When cleaned it was found to be dated 1698, whereas most fenders of its type had previously been assigned to the neighbourhood of the second quarter of the eighteenth century. This important item was given by Messrs Pratt & Son to the Victoria and Albert Museum. Illustrations of it appeared in *The Connoisseur*, March, 1948, p. 57.

46 I quoted from memory; actually this delectable bloomer was made anent the Young Pretender, which was, of course, even less accurate. (*vide* 'The latest batch of British examination papers, reported to the *University Correspondent*,' and quoted in *The Independent*, New York, 1st February, 1912).

47 I do not know whence he got this story; it may be of a sort which crops up in various localities. Mr Desborough tells me that he has heard it told of Devonshire.

48 Information from Mr Charles Partridge, F.S.A., to the late Fred Roe, R.I., in 1937 and 1941.

49 Fred Roe, R.I.: *Old Oak Furniture* (1905), pp. 286-298.

50 Charles R. Beard: *The Romance of Treasure Trove* (1933), pp. 10-12.

51 *Daily Telegraph*, 20th May, 1909.

52 By way of corrective, we may here remind ourselves of a more practical use of good timber: the memorable case, as recorded in Bridges' *Northamptonshire*, of the Drydens' seat at Canons Ashby, wherein a room, 30 ft. long upon 20 ft. wide, was reported to have been entirely floored and wainscoted with the timber of a single oak, grown in that lordship. A last intrusion of the Great House into these pages!

As, of set purpose, technical terms have been reduced to a minimum in this book, there is no point in providing a formal **Glossary**

Certain indispensable terms (*e.g.* chest, coffer, hutch, linenfold, Romayne work) are sufficiently explained in their respective contexts. For the benefit of beginners, the following are added :—

ALMERY (or AMBRY, AUMBRY; *Fr.* ARMOIRE)—A Press or 'Cupboard'. Also used of a doored compartment or recess in a wall (*e.g.* for the Reservation of the Blessed Sacrament in Churches).

CABRIOLE—A term of various applications. Of furniture, used of legs of curved formation, usually ending in bun-, club-, claw-and-ball, hoof-, lion-paw and other types of feet. Related to certain earlier types of curved leg, the cabriole (*i.e.* 'goat-leap') attained its full popularity in the eighteenth century. In countryside pieces (*e.g.* Settles) it survived in debased form to a late period of the century.

CREDENCE-CUPBOARD—An enclosed and doored structure on tall supports, and often provided with a shelf at the base. Related to the Credence-Table, elsewhere described.

GLASS PICTURES—(not to be confused with Glass Paintings). Engravings laid down, after preparation, on glass, after which the bulk of the paper was peeled from the back, and the print varnished and strongly coloured by hand. (See, *inter al.*, H. G. Clarke: *The Story of Glass Pictures* 1690-1810 (*ca.* 1929), and two pamphlets by L. Loewenthal: *Pictures on Glass* (1928), and *Concerning Glass Pictures* (1929). Beginners are warned that there are many fake Glass Pictures, detectable by their poor colour and 'foxy' tone.

GUILLOCHE—Ornament consisting of a succession of circular motifs, somewhat resembling entwined ribbons, frequently present on Elizabethan and seventeenth-century furniture of so-called 'Jacobean' design.

HAKE—In the sense here used, a Pothook or Kettle-hanger, usually adjustable, suspended over the fire. (To obviate misunderstanding, may I add that I use 'kettle' in the old sense implied in the saying 'a pretty kettle of fish'. The Tea-kettle was a late-comer to the Hake.)

KNOPPED (*i.e.* Knobbed)—A member, such as a support, with one or more swelling protuberances.

LATON (LATTEN)—Strictly, a kind of brass, but often used loosely. We may remind ourselves of the anecdote of Ben Jonson at the baptism of one of Shakespeare's children: 'I will give it a Latin spoon, and you shall translate it'. (Another version gives 'Lattin spoones'.)

LUNETTE—In the sense of this book, semicircular ornament, the arched space often enclosing other ornament, and the Spandrels (*q.v.*) being frequently filled as well. Lunette-ornament was very prevalent in the seventeenth century, and especially about the middle of that period.

MITRED MOULDINGS—Mouldings so cut as to form a right-angled joint, thus approximating in shape to an ecclesiastical mitre of early type. The term 'mitre' is similarly used of corner-joins in needlework.

NONSUCH (NONESUCH)—Furniture of sixteenth- and seventeenth-century date, inlaid with architectural views, variously supposed to represent the Palace of Nonesuch at Ewell, or Nonsuch House on Old London Bridge. Neither theory (the latter was first advanced by my father) is proven, and in any case the type is normally a 'town' one.

SKILLET—Metal Cook-Pot, with handle and usually with short legs. A species of early Saucepan, in use medievally, though many examples belong to later period, and are sometimes dated.

SPANDREL—Triangular space between the spring of an arch and an upright, or between two or more adjoining arches or lunettes (*q.v.*).

SPLAT—Back-support of a Chair, linking top and base of a chair-back, in the case of single splats at its middle point.

STRAPWORK—Strips of formal carving, sometimes said to be based on the idea of highly conventionalized entwined or plaited straps; but the latter derivation is, in many cases, somewhat fanciful. Frequently present on Elizabethan and seventeenth-century furniture of so-called 'Jacobean' design. (*cp.* GUILLOCHE).

TESTER—Roof or canopy, especially of a bedstead.

TRENCHER SALT—Squat form of Salt-Cellar for general table use, as opposed to more spectacular pieces such as the Steeple Salt.

TRUNK—As used in this book: (*a*) a form of Chest, including the familiar Travelling Trunk, as elsewhere discussed; (*b*) the centre-part, or pendulum-case, of a long-case clock.

WHORL—Circular ornament enclosing other ornament, sometimes consisting of rays; a decorative roundel enclosing conventional ornament.

Index

Index

Numerals in heavy type refer to figure numbers of plates which appear between pages 32-33 and 96-97. When studying the plates please refer to the full descriptions on pages 12-16.

Index

Index

Index

* I am not denying the manufacture of little tables for children when I say that, in my opinion, a recent theory seemingly seeking to re-class *all* square joined stools as children's tables is exaggerated.—F.G.R.